P9-BAS-896

Christian Caregiving—a Way of Life is a practical, readable, and relevant how-to book that deals with real issues. It has shown me how I can be more thoughtful, patient, and self-aware as I care for others.

Susan Bloomfield
Dean of Admission and Outreach
Raleigh, North Carolina

Christian Caregiving—a Way of Life moves people from the pew to extend God's care out in the world. It's a handbook for how to form caring Christian relationships and put ministry into action.

Jim Guelzow
Pastor
Tampa, Florida

This book is amazing! I've always thought of myself as a fix-it type, but reading this has helped me look at how I relate to people in a new light. The idea that we're the caregivers while God is the Curegiver takes so much pressure off and helps me in many different areas of my life.

Montique Williams
Fitness & Nutrition Coach
Roseville, California

I've found *Christian Caregiving—a Way of Life* an important book to keep handy so I can come back to it again and again. The way it mixes the spiritual side of things with the everyday application makes it so useful. Most importantly, it encourages you to always keep God at the forefront of your caring.

Anita Barnes
Director of Human Resources
Broken Arrow, Oklahoma

Before I read *Christian Caregiving—a Way of Life*, I sometimes found it awkward to use caring tools like prayer, Scripture, and forgiveness. Now, I'm much more confident in my ability to provide care in a distinctively Christian way.

Fung Ying Kwan
Registered Nurse
Shanghai, China

Everybody has a burden they're carrying, and this book gives you the tools to be the person others need when they're in pain. It reaffirms the importance of listening without trying to give advice. Most of all, it reminds you that God is the one who heals—and helps you truly show God's love.

Mary Shaw
Pastor
Haskell, Arkansas

If someone wants to know more about what it means to live out the Christian life, I recommend this book. It's done so much to help me grow in faith.

Mick Petersen
Realtor
Toledo, Ohio

If you've ever wanted to help hurting people but didn't know what to say, *Christian Caregiving—a Way of Life* is the book to read. It contains solid psychological principles and theological truths—and then goes beyond theory to give concrete examples that apply those concepts in the real world.

Andrea Larson, MD
Assisting Pastor
Silverton, Oregon

CHRISTIAN CAREGIVING

A WAY
OF LIFE

SECOND EDITION

ALSO BY KENNETH C. HAUGK

Don't Sing Songs to a Heavy Heart: How to Relate to Those Who Are Suffering

Speaking the Truth in Love: How to Be an Assertive Christian (with Ruth N. Koch)

When and How to Use Mental Health Resources: A Stephen Ministry Guide (with Issac B. Akers)

Antagonists in the Church: How to Identify and Deal with Destructive Conflict

Antagonists in the Church Study Guide (with Amity V. Haugk)

Caring for Inactive Members: How to Make God's House a Home

Reopening the Back Door: Answers to Questions about Ministering to Inactive Members

Discovering God's Vision for Your Life: You and Your Spiritual Gifts

Journeying through Grief:

- *A Time to Grieve*

- *Experiencing Grief*

- *Finding Hope and Healing*

- *Rebuilding and Remembering*

The Quest for Quality Caring

Leader Killers: How to Identify and Deal with Antagonists in Your Organization

Cancer—Now What? Taking Action, Finding Hope, and Navigating the Journey Ahead

CHRISTIAN CAREGIVING

A WAY OF LIFE

SECOND EDITION

KENNETH C. HAUGK, Ph.D.

FOREWORD BY JOEL P. BRETSCHER

STEPHEN MINISTRIES • ST. LOUIS, MISSOURI

CHRISTIAN CAREGIVING—A WAY OF LIFE

Copyright © 2020 by Stephen Ministries St. Louis. All rights reserved.
Originally published in 1984 by Augsburg Publishing House
Second edition 2020

ISBN: 978-1-930445-08-6

Library of Congress Catalog Card Number: 2019952883

Scripture quotations, unless otherwise noted, are taken from the Holy Bible, NEW INTERNATIONAL VERSION®, NIV® Copyright © 1973, 1978, 1984, 2011 by Biblica, Inc.® Used by permission. All rights reserved worldwide.

No portion of this publication may be reproduced, stored in a retrieval system, or transmitted in any form or by any means—whether electronic, mechanical, photocopying, recording, or otherwise—except for brief quotations in articles or reviews, without the prior written permission of the publisher. For permission write to:

Stephen Ministries Permissions Department
2045 Innerbelt Business Center Drive
St. Louis, Missouri 63114-5765

Printed in the U.S.A.

20

1

To all those seeking to make distinctively Christian caring an essential part of their lives

CONTENTS

Foreword 9

Preface 11

1. God as the Curegiver 13

2. God's Constant Presence 19

3. Reaching Spiritual Depths 29

4. Servanthood vs. Servitude 43

5. Tools of Your Trade: Their Use and Abuse 53

6. Prayer 63

7. The Bible 79

8. The Gift of Forgiveness 85

9. Sharing a Blessing 101

10. A Cup of Cold Water 107

11. The Evangelism–Caring Connection 113

12. Celebrate Results—but Focus on the Process 121

13. Hope-Full Caregiving 133

14. Called to Care 141

Notes 145

About the Author 147

FOREWORD

I first read *Christian Caregiving—a Way of Life* when I was training to become a Stephen Minister along with 21 other members of my church in Phoenix, Arizona. *Christian Caregiving* laid the Christ-centered foundation for the one-to-one caring ministry we would provide to hurting people in our congregation and community.

A few years later, I reread the book on a flight to St. Louis for a job interview with Stephen Ministries. I was excited about the possibility of joining the staff of an organization that empowers high-quality ministry in thousands of congregations, as well as meeting Dr. Kenneth Haugk, the book's author and the founder and Executive Director of Stephen Ministries. That interview began a working relationship and friendship that I still enjoy and value today.

After moving to St. Louis, I read it again—this time as a Stephen Leader at my new church, when my pastor and I were co-teaching our congregation's first class of 19 Stephen Ministers. The concepts of distinctively Christian care struck a chord with them and have infused their ministry—both as Stephen Ministers and elsewhere in the church. In Phoenix, in St. Louis, or anywhere else, Christian caregiving truly becomes a way of life.

I read the book a fourth time when both of my children were in high school and I was asked to teach relational skills to our church youth group. The class helped our teens incorporate the concepts and skills of *Christian Caregiving* into their lives.

Every time I read this book, I appreciate its down-to-earth practicality. *Christian Caregiving—a Way of Life* is a how-to manual that presents tangible ways we can be Christ to others every day—active listening, relating to deep spiritual needs, sharing a blessing, building a prayer, offering a cup of cold water, and other powerful tools of care.

Ken Haugk is uniquely qualified to have written this book. Holding a Ph.D. in clinical psychology, he practiced psychotherapy and taught psychology for many years. In addition, he's an ordained pastor and served both in a congregation and as a seminary professor. Drawing on this background and Dr. Haugk's passion to equip God's people for the work of ministry (Ephesians 4:12), *Christian Caregiving—a Way of Life* blends sound psychology with biblical theology to provide ideas and suggestions that anyone can put into action.

Over the years, more than a million people have read this book—as part of a small group or on their own. I welcome you to this growing wave of readers who are making this book's Christ-centered principles and practices a way of life.

Joel P. Bretscher
Program Director
Stephen Ministries
St. Louis, Missouri

PREFACE

Pain and suffering are a fact of life. Wherever you are, there are likely to be people who are hurting physically, emotionally, relationally, or spiritually—people who need to experience the love of Christ.

Too often, though, the distinctiveness of the care we can offer as Christians goes unidentified and unexpressed. As a result, care that is uniquely Christian is rarer than it should be. That's why I wrote this book.

Christian Caregiving—a Way of Life has a twofold purpose:

1) to define, describe, and elevate *distinctively Christian caring,* and

2) to explain how such caring can become a *way of life* for followers of Christ.

This book is a resource for those who wonder, "How can my Christian faith make a difference as I relate with and care for other people?"

Christian Caregiving—a Way of Life is a how-to manual dealing with real-life issues in caring and relating. The Christian perspective behind the book is like that of C. S. Lewis's *Mere Christianity:* a grassroots faith common to all Christians.

I write from the standpoint that both Christianity and the field of mental health have important roles to play in caregiving. Christian caregivers need to be empowered and affirmed, but not at the expense of the valuable contributions of psychology and the other arts and sciences. The world needs all the caring it can get—from psychology *and* theology.

When I originally wrote this book, the need for distinctively Christian caregiving was both vital and urgent, and the same is true today. I hope that as you read this book, you will be uplifted and caught up in the vision it offers for making this approach to caring a central part of your life.

GOD AS THE CUREGIVER

Farmers teach lessons in hope every day. They toil for weeks, preparing the soil for planting. Tilling, fertilizing, planting seeds, cultivating . . . all these activities serve to prepare and nourish the crop. Every day, farmers hope—for rain, but not too much; for sun, but not too much; for warmth, but not too much. When the harvest arrives, farmers are gathering *hopes fulfilled* as much as *work rewarded.*

The apostle Paul knew this when he wrote, "I planted the seed, Apollos watered it, but God made it grow. So neither he who plants nor he who waters is anything, but only God, who makes things grow" (1 Corinthians 3:6–7). Just as a farmer prepares and nourishes a crop for harvest, so the Christian caregiver plants and waters. God then provides the growth. In other words, *Christians are responsible for care; God is responsible for cure.*

The role of a Christian caregiver is to prepare the soil for the Great Curegiver. This means helping create the necessary conditions for change and healing for the care receiver—and then waiting expectantly and prayerfully on the Lord. When you provide care for hurting people, you participate in Christian therapy, establishing a favorable environment where God will bring about transformation and growth in his wisdom and timing.

The word *therapy* is derived from the Greek *therapeuo*, which has two related meanings:

- **to serve**—"to render assistance or help by performing certain duties . . . to serve, to render service," and

- **to heal**—"to cause someone to recover health, often with the implication of having taken care of such a person—to heal, to cure, to take care of, healing."[1]

The first meaning is relational, focusing on the process of serving, caring, and preparing another person for healing. Therapeutic processes are actions the *caregiver* can perform, like listening, empathizing, and helping people talk through their feelings. In this sense, anyone involved in caring for another person is providing therapy.

The second meaning is more results-oriented, focusing on outcomes in the care receiver's life. Those healing outcomes—such as peace, calm, restoration, redemption, and salvation—are beyond our control. In the New Testament, they are never attributed to the abilities or wisdom of ordinary humans; they always come from God, the *Curegiver*.

As Christian caregivers, we recognize that our role is to focus on the process of serving and caring (the first meaning of *therapeuo*) while we leave the outcome of healing and redemption (the second meaning) to God. This is what makes Christian care distinctive. While all caregivers establish relationships to serve people in need, Christian caregivers trust in God for the results. Living out this knowledge—that results belong to God—is living in faith. Such faith has benefits for both the caregiver and the person receiving care.

FREEDOM FOR THE CAREGIVER

When you as caregiver realize that God is the Curegiver, you are freed from false expectations. You don't need to pressure yourself for results or place unrealistic demands on the other person to change or get better. Instead, you can concentrate on creating the best therapeutic conditions for growth and healing to occur: being fully present, communicating acceptance and love, and helping the one receiving care explore his or her thoughts and feelings.

Not relying on God for the results can lead to two pitfalls. First, you can end up relying on yourself to get the desired results, pressuring the other person to grow or change. When results don't seem to be happening, or don't happen as quickly as you'd like, you may feel weighed down by the responsibility, worry about the lack of results, and begin to doubt your ability as a caregiver. This cycle of worry and doubt can turn your focus further inward and make it more difficult to focus on and care for the other person.

Second, you can find yourself placing responsibility for success on the one receiving care. At first, this may feel freeing, since you're not holding yourself responsible for results. Eventually, however, this approach will leave both you and the care receiver frustrated, as it puts unrealistic expectations on the care receiver. Although God has provided humans with many inner resources for coping and changing, people who are hurting cannot simply make themselves get better, nor should you expect them to do so. What they need is to experience Christian care and the healing power of God.

When you trust God to provide results, you are freed from the pressure you might otherwise put on yourself or the care receiver. This freedom is not a license to be lax in caregiving; instead, it allows you to focus on the process while leaving the results to God. Being a good caregiver, like being a good farmer, takes effort. While that effort doesn't always guarantee the results you want, it gives care receivers the best opportunity to experience hope and healing.

FREEDOM FOR THE CARE RECEIVER

The person receiving care also benefits when you understand that God is the Curegiver. He or she won't be weighed down by unrealistic expectations but rather is free to receive Christ's love through your care, working through difficult thoughts and feelings at a pace suited to the individual. At the right time, the person receiving care will be able to risk change and growth, trusting God to provide the cure.

This is good news for the care receiver, because he or she has plenty of responsibilities and challenges without the added burden of meeting expectations for results. To begin with, the person's normal daily responsibilities never really go away. Then, there is the circumstance or issue that has caused the need for care. On top of that, just needing care puts a person in a vulnerable position. Someone facing this tremendous pressure doesn't need to be burdened with the additional expectation to get better on someone else's timetable.

Focusing on the process of caring and leaving the results to God frees both the caregiver and the care receiver from the responsibility to generate a positive outcome fast. This doesn't mean the care receiver can become passive and simply let the crisis take over. Rather, it means he or she can invest in the process by expressing feelings, sharing openly, being honest, and accepting care—all the while trusting that God will work through that process to bring healing.

In chapter 12, "Celebrate Results—but Focus on the Process," you will learn about what can happen when you care in a distinctively Christian way. For now, it's enough to know whom those results come from. They come from the Lord—the same Lord who is your Shepherd, who walks with you through the valley of the shadow of death. When you realize that God is the Curegiver, you are free to accept the responsibility to care, the care receiver will be free to receive the help you offer, and both of you will find the caring process much easier to bear.

GOD'S CONSTANT
PRESENCE

Driver's education classes help students learn to drive in a safe setting with an experienced driving instructor. Once students have learned how to operate a vehicle, they get behind the wheel and begin driving, with the instructor keeping a close eye on their performance and offering input and feedback. Often, the car is fitted with dual controls so the instructor can take control of the car whenever necessary.

It can be many months before a new driver is fully licensed and ready to venture out on the road independently. Even after reaching that milestone, drivers can still benefit from having someone in the car with them to help keep an eye on the road and spot any potential hazards. There is comfort and freedom in knowing that you are not alone.

In the same way, it's comforting and empowering to know that you're never alone as a Christian caregiver. God is always present, reaching out through you to the care receiver, even if you're not fully aware of it. This is part of the distinctiveness of Christian care.

HOW IS GOD PRESENT?

God is with you at *all* times, including your caregiving. Here are three ways you may experience God's presence in the caring process.

LIKE AN ATTENDING SURGEON

An attending surgeon instructs and supervises surgical residents in training. Before a resident enters the operating room, the attending surgeon makes sure he or she is fully prepared for the operation. The attending surgeon then remains fully available for the resident, directly overseeing the operation and offering ongoing guidance throughout the resident's work. Should a situation occur where a resident needs support, the attending surgeon can talk the resident through the procedure, assist in the operation, or even step in to complete the surgery. One could say that the attending surgeon's wisdom and experience find expression in the resident's hands.

God's presence is often like that of an attending surgeon as you relate to and care for others. It may be your hands that do the work, but God is with you, guiding your hands through his wisdom. With God watching over you like an attending surgeon, you have powerful and distinctively Christian support.

LIKE A WOUNDED HEALER

Another way God may be experienced in a caring relationship is as a *wounded healer.*[1] In Jesus, an all-knowing, all-powerful, and everywhere-present God has made himself like us and taken upon himself all the evil, pain, and suffering we face in life.

> But he was pierced for our transgressions, he was crushed for our iniquities; the punishment that brought us peace was on him, and by his wounds we are healed (Isaiah 53:5).

Here we encounter the wondrous paradox that God is not only the attending surgeon with great wisdom and confident presence—he is also the patient. Jesus speaks of this:

> "For I was hungry and you gave me something to eat, I was thirsty and you gave me something to drink, I was a stranger and you invited me in, I needed clothes and you clothed me, I was sick and you looked after me, I was in prison and you came to visit me" (Matthew 25:35–36).

The people ask when they did this for him. His answer: "'I tell you the truth, whatever you did for one of the least of these brothers of mine, you did for me'" (Matthew 25:40).

Jesus is the wounded healer, both the patient and the Great Physician. Christ is present in you as you care for others *and* in those who receive your care. He has been there himself. He knows what suffering is all about. And he knows how to bring healing.

LIKE A COMFORTABLE CHAIR

I once saw an *art nouveau* chair that symbolizes another way God is present in caring relationships. The chair was soft and comfortable, and it had the outline of a hand painted on the seat and arms. It seemed to invite you to relax in its palm.

God's presence is like that. Jesus promises, "'No one can snatch [my followers] out of my hand'" (John 10:28b). He provides all the warmth and comfort of your favorite chair as he reminds you that he holds you, the care receiver, the situation, and the whole world in his hands. An old Irish blessing expresses this:

> May the road rise up to meet you.
> May the wind be always at your back.
> May the sun shine warm upon your face,
> the rains fall soft upon your fields,
> and until we meet again,
> may God hold you in the palm of his hand.

WAYS TO RECOGNIZE GOD'S PRESENCE

God is present at all times, whether or not we realize it—but cultivating a greater awareness of God's presence in your caregiving can give you the courage and confidence you need to minister most effectively to the hurting person. Here are some ways to recognize and acknowledge God's presence in your caregiving.

THROUGH PRAYER

Prayer can draw your attention to God's presence in your life and in your caring. Before you meet with the care receiver, you can pray for an awareness of God's presence and guidance. Then, if it seems appropriate and the other person is open to it, you might offer to pray for him or her while you're together. In between the times you meet, you can pray for the person to be aware of God's presence and to experience God's healing.

The more you bring prayer into these relationships, the more you will recognize and acknowledge God's presence in your caregiving—and the more distinctively Christian your care will be.

THROUGH A HEIGHTENED CONSCIOUSNESS OF GOD'S PRESENCE

Another way to remain aware of God's presence is to actively cultivate your consciousness of being in God's company at all times.

Brother Lawrence was a 17th-century monk who worked in the kitchen of a Carmelite monastery in Paris, France. In the midst of his daily work, Brother Lawrence sought to develop and maintain a continual awareness of God's presence. His superior, Abbe Joseph de Beaufort, took notice of Brother Lawrence's unusual wisdom and arranged a series of interviews with him to learn more about his approach to life. Those conversations, along with a number of Brother Lawrence's letters and other writings, make up the book *Practicing the Presence of God.*

Here, Brother Lawrence describes how he approached his daily kitchen duty:

> At the beginning of my duties, I said to God with a son-like trust, "My God, since You are with me, and since it is Your will that I should apply my mind to these outward things, I pray that You will give me the grace to remain with You and keep company with You. But so that my work may be better, Lord, work with me; receive my work and possess all my affections." Finally, during my work, I continued to speak to Him in a familiar way, offering Him my little services, and asking for His grace. At the end of my work, I examined how I had done it, and if I found any good in it, I thanked God. . . . [B]y doing many little acts of love, I came to a state in which it would be as difficult for me not to think of God as it had

been difficult to accustom myself to think of Him at the beginning.[2]

Although few achieve the level of awareness that Brother Lawrence experienced, any of us can grow in our awareness of God's presence by simply turning our attention toward God on a regular basis. God is always present in our lives and caring relationships, but a heightened consciousness of God's presence can cultivate an attitude of trust in him.

BY VERBALIZING GOD'S PRESENCE

We can also come alive to God's presence in a powerful way by actually mentioning the fact of his presence. It's like visiting an art museum. If you were to walk unaccompanied through the museum, you may find yourself drawn to the beauty of the works on display. However, if you were to tour the museum with a guide who could talk knowledgably about the artists, their times, their techniques, and the meanings behind their creations, your appreciation for the same works of art would most likely grow significantly.

The same is true in a caring relationship. God is always there and can be experienced even when he is not specifically identified or discussed. When you openly and appropriately address his presence in that caring relationship, however, it can open up new perspectives and avenues of caring.

Years ago, I had a client who was nearing the end of her psychotherapy when a serious crisis occurred in her life. I was concerned that this crisis might affect her adversely, perhaps throwing her into an emotional tailspin—but it didn't happen. She experienced sadness, anxiety, and frustration with the situation as anyone would, but she was able to handle the crisis extremely well.

This confirmed that the change and growth she had experienced through therapy had made a lasting difference in her life. I remember saying to her, "It seems as if we've done our work well."

She smiled and said:

> I think it was really God who did it. There were times when I felt so low, so despondent, so out of control that I didn't know what to do. I have an idea that at those times you didn't know what to do with me either. I really believe that God was with me when neither I nor you knew what to do—that God was the one providing the therapy during those times. I think we both have done a good job. You have been a good therapist to me and I have worked very hard myself. I've taken a lot of risks and shared with you a lot of scary and personal things about myself. But we need to give credit where credit is due, and that is with God.

What a tremendous profession of faith that was! She testified that God was present—helping, guiding, and comforting both me as caregiver and her as care receiver throughout the caring relationship. So it is with you.

REACHING
SPIRITUAL DEPTHS

Christian caregivers are uniquely qualified to provide Christ-centered care that addresses people's deep spiritual needs. While they typically provide support to address emotional and other types of needs, the element of spiritual care helps to set Christ-centered care apart.

Whatever a person's beliefs or relationship with God, difficult experiences in life can stir up challenging spiritual questions:

- What is the meaning of life?

- Why am I here?

- Is there a God, and if so, does God care about me?

- What's my purpose in life?

- What is right, and what is wrong?

- Why does God allow suffering?

- Why do we have to die?

These kinds of questions are all valid. They're part of the flow of human life, and they point to genuine spiritual concerns that anyone might have. Even people with strong faith struggle with questions like these. As a Christian caregiver, you have a unique opportunity to minister to this spiritual dimension of people's concerns along with their other needs.

CHALLENGES IN MINISTERING TO SPIRITUAL NEEDS

Christian caregivers are sometimes reluctant to address the spiritual needs of those receiving care. A few of the main reasons are listed here. Understanding these reasons can help you move beyond any hesitancy you may feel and provide effective spiritual care for people who need it.

WIDELY DIFFERING RELIGIOUS BELIEFS

One reason people are reluctant to introduce faith into their caregiving is due to the diversity of religious belief and non-belief in the world today. People are increasingly aware that they can't presume everyone will have religious beliefs similar to their own.

With such a wide range of religious perspectives, the people we care for may speak a different faith language than we do. Even those who are Christian can have widely diverging views about God, faith, and the Christian life. This means it can feel risky to care for others' spiritual needs.

Of course, it's important to be sensitive to the reality that the person we're caring for may have different beliefs than we do. But this doesn't mean we need to avoid conversations about spiritual needs—far from it! We can offer Christ-centered care while also being sensitive to and respectful of the other person's religious beliefs. The material in this chapter and the rest of the book can help you do so.

CONCERNS ABOUT POSSIBLE ANIMOSITY TOWARD CHRISTIANITY

Along with the increasing recognition of religious diversity are growing concerns about possible animosity toward Christianity. Some Christians may be reluctant to identify spiritual issues and address spiritual needs in their caregiving because they assume that others will react strongly and negatively to any such conversation.

While there may be exceptions, most people are generally open to conversations about spirituality and faith as long as they know they won't be pressured to believe or act in a certain way. When people are hurting, they tend to be more aware of their spiritual needs and more willing to explore them with someone they trust to listen without pressuring, shaming, or judging them.

FEELINGS OF INADEQUACY

Christians may also be reluctant to engage in conversations about spiritual needs because they don't think they're up to the task, perhaps believing they aren't spiritual enough, knowledgeable enough, or *Christian* enough. Since none of us is perfect, some feelings of inadequacy are understandable. In this case, though, they're based on a misunderstanding of what it means to be a Christian caregiver—an assumption that it's about having and imparting the right spiritual answers.

When it comes to addressing spiritual needs in the context of a caring relationship, your role is not to persuade the other person or pass along great spiritual wisdom. Instead, you're called to listen, empathize, help the other person talk through feelings, share Christian resources at appropriate times, and above all to trust that God is at work in and through you to bring hope and healing. That's something any Christian can do and grow in.

OTHERS' HESITATION TO TALK ABOUT SPIRITUAL NEEDS

Faith is often considered a private matter between a person and God, and discussing faith with others may leave people feeling vulnerable. As a result, people may be hesitant to talk about spiritual needs and reveal any spiritual questions or doubts. Knowing that people can be uncomfortable talking about spiritual needs, caregivers may likewise be reluctant to bring them up. They may wonder whether the relationship is close enough and trusting enough for the other person to risk sharing.

Those are all natural concerns. However, without someone being willing to open the door to a spiritual conversation, the hurting person's spiritual needs are likely to be neglected.

OPENING THE DOOR FOR SPIRITUAL TALK

As a caring Christian, it's important that you open the door for the care receiver to express his or her spiritual needs. Here are some ways you can initiate and encourage communication about spiritual issues or questions.

PROVIDE AN ATMOSPHERE OF ACCEPTANCE

To help people overcome their reluctance to talk about spirituality, you'll need to establish an atmosphere of acceptance. That doesn't mean you'll necessarily agree with or have no concerns about what the other person says. Rather, it means helping the person feel free to share whatever he or she is thinking and feeling, making it clear that you won't do any lecturing, criticizing, or judging.

The other person needs to know it's safe to express any spiritual questions and doubts with you.

The key to establishing an atmosphere of acceptance is to listen fully, being especially attentive to the person's hurts and struggles. You might be one of the few who allow the person to share real spiritual concerns without interrupting or trying to change his or her mind. As trust develops, the person will be able to share more openly and freely. Your appropriate and sensitive use of resources like prayer and the Bible can also contribute to an atmosphere of acceptance and let the person know it's perfectly all right to share spiritual concerns with you. (Chapters 6 and 7 provide more information about using these two resources.)

BE ALERT TO SPIRITUAL NEEDS

In addition to creating an atmosphere of acceptance, you'll also need to be alert to detecting the other person's spiritual needs. That includes both expressed and unexpressed needs—even if someone never talks directly about God, faith, or any other spiritual matter, he or she may still have significant spiritual needs.

Being alert to what people feel, think, and say is important. Your ability to discern the spiritual dimension in the life of a care receiver can help you hear and respond to a hidden cry for help from someone in a spiritual crisis.

ENCOURAGE PEOPLE TO DISCUSS SPIRITUAL NEEDS

The author of Proverbs wrote, "The purposes of a man's heart are deep waters, but a man of understanding draws them out" (20:5). Just as people need encouragement to express their feelings and needs in other areas of life, they also need encouragement to talk about their spiritual needs.

When caring for someone, you will probably ask general questions like, "How are you feeling?" or "How are things going?" or "What would you like to see happen in the future?" Similar questions can also be asked about the person's spiritual life:

- "How has this situation affected your view of God?"

- "What kind of spiritual background did you have growing up?"

- "How has your faith changed over time?"

- "What role does faith play in your life?"

- "What values are important to you?"

Another way to encourage people to share their spiritual needs is to invite them to say more about something specific they've mentioned to you. Here are some examples:

- "You mentioned that you've wondered whether your suffering is God's way of punishing you. Could you say more about that?"

- "A few minutes ago you said you don't really have anything to look forward to right now. Tell me more about that."

- "You said you don't really think religion has anything to offer you. Could you tell me more about what you're thinking?"

Sometimes, the person you're caring for may try to avoid talking about spiritual matters by responding with a general statement like, "I guess God knows best," or "I've gone to church my whole life," or "I know God is in control." These statements don't really address how the person *feels* about his or her relationship to God. To move beyond broad statements and get into true feelings, you may need to ask some follow-up questions that encourage the individual to share more openly. This part of a conversation shows how that might be done.

Caregiver: You're facing some major surgery tomorrow. I'm wondering what you're thinking and feeling about that.

Care receiver: I guess I'm more than a little nervous, but I trust the surgeon. I'm probably as ready as I'll ever be.

Caregiver: I see. How are you feeling spiritually?

Care receiver: Well, I've always been a Christian. I never miss church if I can help it.

Caregiver: That's true. I'm wondering, though, how you're feeling about God during all this.

Care receiver: I mean, I'm sure God will be with me tomorrow.

Caregiver: Could you say more about what you mean?

Care receiver (fidgeting): Well, my life is in God's hands. He'll do what he wants to do, and there's nothing I can do about it, right? All I can do is trust him.

Caregiver: How are you feeling about that?

Care receiver (dispiritedly): I don't know. I'd be surprised if he's paying much attention. God has a lot more important things to worry about than me.

Caregiver: Tell me more about that.

In this example, the caregiver's gentle persistence has opened the door for the care receiver to begin sharing about spiritual uncertainties. Now that the care receiver has opened up a little bit, the caregiver can continue to provide an atmosphere of acceptance and a safe place to express those concerns and fears.

TAKE WHATEVER TIME IS NECESSARY FOR EXTENDED CONVERSATION ABOUT SPIRITUAL CONCERNS

Occasionally, you and the other person might decide to focus in on a specific spiritual concern and spend more time discussing it. You might even choose to have multiple conversations around a particular spiritual issue.

For example, suppose you're talking with a man who has been diagnosed with cancer. He's told you about his struggles to understand everything he's going through in light of his Christian faith. He'll probably need to talk extensively about a range of thoughts and feelings connected with his illness and relationship with God. As a caregiver, you'll want to allow plenty of time to listen actively and come to understand his faith struggles. Since this is a personal, sensitive matter, the man's anxiety and tension will probably intensify as he explores his feelings. By taking the time to listen, understand, and empathize, you can help him gain new insights into his relationship with God and grow in his faith, even as he struggles with his situation.

PITFALLS TO AVOID

There are some common pitfalls that can come up in ministering to others' spiritual needs. By avoiding these problems in relating, you'll significantly increase your effectiveness as a caring person.

PITFALL: ONE-WAY DISCUSSIONS

One of the dangers of discussing spiritual concerns is that the discussion can easily become a one-way flow of words from the caregiver to the care receiver. The caregiver might at first be responding well to the needs and feelings of the person receiving care, but when a spiritual question is raised, the caregiver could be tempted to shift into the role of a lecturer. When this happens, the conversation quickly becomes a monologue in which the caregiver does most of the talking, potentially in a way that comes across as condescending.

A conversation about spiritual needs should be a dialogue, involving a mutual exploration of spiritual feelings and needs. Talking about God or faith is not about taking a funnel and pouring the right thoughts into someone's head. It's a sharing process in which you will both speak and listen—and in fact, as a caregiver, you'll want to do much more listening than speaking.

PITFALL: PRESSURING

As a Christian, you may have a strong desire to see the person you're caring for embrace certain thoughts, feelings, and beliefs. You might hope for the person to feel and express complete faith in God or think and act in ways that are consistent with your own beliefs. That's natural.

As a caregiver, however, you need to avoid pressuring the person to think, feel, or act in particular ways. Pressure threatens the person's boundaries and short-circuits the caring process, which can lead him or her to become defensive and possibly end the conversation or even the relationship. This is an area where Christian caregivers especially need to focus on the process of care and trust God, the Curegiver, for results.

PITFALL: RELIGIOUS CLICHÉS

Often when people don't know what to say to those who are struggling spiritually, they end up repeating common, pithy sayings that seem to fit the situation—but that in reality aren't all that helpful. Some examples of these religious clichés and pat phrases are:

- "Everything happens for a reason."

- "When God closes a door, he opens a window."

- "God doesn't give you any more than you can handle."

- "It's God's will."

Although such clichés might sometimes contain some truth, they usually hurt much more than they help when a person is going through a difficult time. Clichés offer little insight, shut off meaningful conversation, and leave the hurting person feeling like others don't really understand.

If you're not sure what to say, it's better to say that you aren't sure what to say than to resort to a cliché. When people are hurting, they don't need pithy religious sayings; they need someone to listen, empathize, and understand what they're going through. Indeed, sometimes you don't really need to say anything at all; your presence and your willingness to listen actively are often enough.[1]

PITFALL: A KNOW-IT-ALL ATTITUDE

Everyone has opinions. This in itself certainly isn't a bad thing, but problems can arise if a caregiver comes across as a spiritual know-it-all. Even when it's unintentional, such an impression leaves little or no room for the care receiver to explore what he or she really believes and embrace genuine faith. A rigid attitude that pressures a person to simply accept what the caregiver says is likely to yield negative results in the caring relationship.

The first possible outcome, and perhaps the worst, is if the person receiving care passively accepts the caregiver's point of view, rather than thinking it through and coming to his or her own conclusion. Another possibility may be that the care receiver resents the perceived know-it-all attitude and avoids or rejects conversations about spiritual matters entirely. A third could be that the care receiver becomes defensive and starts an argument. None of these outcomes is conducive to spiritual growth.

Everyone's life has a spiritual dimension, which God reveals at unexpected times and places. As one who seeks to care as a Christian, you need to be ready to relate to the deep spiritual needs of others. Your readiness to do so will be communicated to others by the climate of acceptance and encouragement you create, by your sensitivity to opportunities to raise the issue, and by your willingness to take whatever time is necessary. The person you are caring for will find you trustworthy because you listen more than talk and you avoid responding with clichés, pressure, or a lofty, superior manner. Thus, the door will be open for providing care that is deeply and distinctively Christian.

SERVANTHOOD
VS. SERVITUDE

Martin Luther wrote, "The Christian individual is a completely free lord of all, subject to none. The Christian individual is a completely dutiful servant of all, subject to all." [1]

As a Christian, you are called to freedom—not only freedom *from* an obligation to serve but also, more importantly, freedom *to* serve with joy and satisfaction.

People sometimes have misgivings and misunderstanding about this Christian call to servanthood—most often because they confuse *servanthood* with *servitude*. *Servitude* implies bondage, slavery, and involuntary labor. *Servanthood,* on the other hand, indicates willingness, choice, and voluntary commitment.

There is a big difference between servanthood and servitude. Servanthood is acting out of commitment and love; it's healthy and uplifting. Servitude is acting out of duty and fear; it's unhealthy and even demeaning. While servanthood lifts up and benefits everyone involved, servitude actually creates more difficulties—for both the server and the one being served—than no service at all.

When Christians equate servanthood with servitude, they can feel enslaved to their calling rather than freed by it. Under these circumstances, caring becomes an act of servitude.

One reason Christians can become entangled in the web of servitude is an overall fear of not pleasing God. They may think that if they exhaust themselves in service to others, they'll make up for areas where they've fallen short. When people's service comes from this motivation, however, they can end up harming those they mean to help. Acting in servitude often depersonalizes the other person, because the caregiver comes to see the person as a project to complete or a problem to fix rather than a human being who needs care.

Some people believe that Christianity inevitably leads to servitude. On the contrary, the distinctiveness of Christianity helps lead people toward true servanthood. By understanding the differences between servitude and servanthood, we can serve others freely and meaningfully.

To lay out those differences, this chapter looks at four servitude pitfalls and four servanthood alternatives.

Servitude	Servanthood
Overidentification Taking on the other person's problems at the risk of losing your own identity	**Empathy** Feeling with the other person while retaining your identity and objectivity
Superficial Sweetness Compensating for negative feelings by covering them up with cheerfulness	**Genuineness** Being yourself and acting congruently
Being Manipulated Allowing the other person to take advantage of the relationship	**Filling Needs, Not Simply Wants** Being straightforward and assertive, including confronting in a caring way when necessary
Begrudging Care Complaining about the relationship and not wanting to be involved in it	**Intentionality** Choosing whether or not to be in a caring relationship, based on what is best for everyone involved

SERVITUDE PITFALL #1: OVERIDENTIFICATION

When people experience life's challenges, it's often like they're stuck in the mud. Seeing someone in such a plight, it can be tempting to jump in with both feet to help them escape the mudhole.

Jumping right in, though, is overidentifying with the other person. Overidentification is when the caregiver becomes so emotionally entangled with the other person's pains, problems, and emotional burdens that they become the caregiver's own. The caregiver may well achieve emotional solidarity with the other person, but he or she loses the objectivity needed to help the other person out—and may even get stuck in the same pit.

When a caregiver overidentifies with a person needing care, no one benefits. The other person is still in the mudhole, and now the caregiver may need help as well. Misery does indeed love company, but company on its own is not enough to bring help and healing to those experiencing misery.

THE SERVANTHOOD APPROACH: EMPATHY

Walking in the freedom of servanthood, a caring Christian responds to the other person's pain with empathy. Empathy involves experiencing another's problems as if they were your own, without losing the "as if" quality.[2] It entails entering the mudhole carefully and with purpose—getting a solid grip on the root of a nearby tree to help you retain your stability and sense of objectivity as you help the other person out of the mud.

When you empathize, the other person receives effective care, and you avoid being ensnared by his or her situation. You are fully present and maintain the all-important objectivity that enables you to communicate, "Let's get out of this together." With empathy, you firmly grasp the other person's hand to help him or her out of the hole and back onto stable ground.

SERVITUDE PITFALL #2: SUPERFICIAL SWEETNESS

A person who feels reluctant, unwilling, or angry at the prospect of serving may cloak that feeling with an exaggerated and unnatural sweetness. The problem is not the sweetness itself but that it's incongruent; it doesn't match the person's true feelings, which are usually the exact opposite of what's on the surface.

Caregivers displaying artificial sweetness may not be fully aware of that incongruence, so they're unlikely to resolve the issue on their own. While the caregiver is covering his or her true feelings with superficial sweetness, no real connection with the person needing care can take place. The one seeking help would only be relating to a mask.

THE SERVANTHOOD APPROACH: GENUINENESS

The servanthood alternative to superficial sweetness is genuineness. Genuineness stems from congruence with yourself—when your behaviors match your true feelings. That doesn't mean expressing absolutely everything you're thinking and feeling, but it does mean being aware of what's going on inside yourself and acting accordingly. Being genuine is about being who you really are.

Genuineness is disarmingly contagious. As you, the caregiver, set aside your mask, you empower others to do the same. A caregiver's genuineness can be a model and an encouragement for others to shed their masks and be themselves.

Note that genuine, congruent individuals are not universally appreciated. When you truly open up by being genuine, not everyone will respond positively. Some people might resent that you're expressing your true self so comfortably or that you've shattered their illusions. Don't let that stop you. Being a servant is not easy, but the reward of spreading genuineness to others is worth the effort to model it.

SERVITUDE PITFALL #3: BEING MANIPULATED

At times, a person being cared for may be a *manipulator:* someone who seeks to exert psychological influence and control over another person for his or her own purposes. When someone tries to control your behavior or play on your emotions for selfish ends, he or she is trying to manipulate you. A relationship where manipulation goes unchecked ceases to be meaningful or healthy. No genuine relating can occur when one person is treated as an object by another; such a one-sided relationship is no relationship at all.

Sincere, caring Christians can be manipulated by those they serve, possibly without even realizing that manipulation is occurring. At some level, they may recognize that something is wrong, but they view their suffering and endurance of that mistreatment as honorable and Christ-like—as part of the cross they think they are called to bear.

Allowing oneself to be manipulated is not Christian servanthood. It's demeaning to the caregiver, in effect saying, "I am an object at your disposal." It's also demeaning to the manipulator; far from being Christ-like, allowing manipulation to take place allows the manipulator to continue in unhealthy, destructive, and overly dependent behaviors.

THE SERVANTHOOD APPROACH: FILLING NEEDS, NOT SIMPLY WANTS

Part of true Christian servanthood is not allowing yourself to be manipulated. In order to show love for people and build them up, your goal in caring must be to help meet their needs, not simply their wants.

For example, a child might want nothing but ice cream for dinner, but what the child needs is a healthy, balanced diet. The same goes for anyone who is manipulative. Certainly, you should keep a person's wants in mind, but avoid giving in to the person's whims and neglecting his or her true needs.

As much as possible, you'll want to remain warm, caring, and gentle even as you resist manipulation. Nurturing is part of the caring process. But when a person tries to manipulate, it's important not to let yourself become one of the person's objects. Resisting this temptation requires effective, assertive relating skills. A direct, forthright approach is the way to combat manipulation successfully.

SERVITUDE PITFALL #4: BEGRUDGING CARE

Occasionally, people stumble into a relationship they really didn't want anything to do with. Because they feel obliged to care, though, they continue in the situation—all the while complaining, inwardly or outwardly, about the individual and the relationship. The begrudging nature of the relationship is an obstacle to effective caring and relating.

In such a predicament, it's often better to consider ending the situation than to keep participating in it grudgingly. This doesn't mean that if a relationship is difficult, you should simply give up on it. Even in highly challenging caring situations, it's possible to find joy in bearing the burdens of another. But when bitterness replaces joy, it's unlikely that any good will come from the relationship for anyone involved.

THE SERVANTHOOD APPROACH: INTENTIONALITY

When you act with the freedom of servanthood, you consciously choose to enter and continue relationships. That deliberate decision to care lends power to your presence, in stark contrast to unwilling care based on a mistaken sense of obligation.

Even with intentionality, relationships will not always be sparkling and dynamic. Some relationships are more enjoyable and rewarding than others. But when you make a decision to serve, the strength of your commitment will carry you through any less pleasant times.

LIVING IN THE FREEDOM OF SERVANTHOOD

Remember the example of Jesus, from whom distinctively Christian service takes its cue. Our Lord willingly washed his disciples' feet, not as a demeaning task but as an act of selfless love (John 13:1–15). Christ defined servanthood when he said that "'the Son of man came not to be served, but to serve, and to give his life as a ransom for many'" (Matthew 20:28). Following Jesus' model, we too can live in the freedom of servanthood.

TOOLS OF YOUR TRADE:
THEIR USE AND ABUSE

Imagine someone very close to you has died, and you're struggling spiritually in your grief. To help you work through your loss, your congregation sends two people on separate days to provide care for you.

One of the caregivers, Eric, comes to visit first. You mention to Eric that, among other things, you're experiencing spiritual doubts and struggles. Eric expresses sincere care and concern for you, but he doesn't seem open to talking about spiritual issues. Each time you bring up your faith or doubts, Eric changes the subject, so you never really get to explore those struggles together. When it's time for Eric to leave, you ask whether he would mind praying for you. Agreeing reluctantly, he stumbles through a brief, awkward prayer that leaves both of you feeling embarrassed. As he departs, you realize that even though Eric seemed willing to help, he didn't address any of your deepest needs, and you feel disappointed and frustrated.

A couple days later, Amanda, the other caregiver, visits you. When you start to mention the spiritual struggles you're having, Amanda begins quoting Bible verses at you. Then, without taking time to listen and understand what you're going through, she launches into her thoughts on the doctrine of the resurrection, reciting a well-rehearsed dissertation on how God, through Jesus, has removed the sting of death. As your visit is wrapping up, Amanda offers a lengthy but very general prayer on death and resurrection that has no reference to your specific needs. You know Amanda means well, but you feel ignored, demeaned, and hurt by her actions. You're relieved when she concludes her lecturing and walks out the door.

Neither Eric nor Amanda offered effective Christian care. Although Eric expressed natural human concern, he didn't offer distinctively Christian care, leaving spiritual needs un-addressed and even ignored. Amanda was quick to share her knowledge of the Bible and theology, but she didn't use those tools to care in a sensitive, helpful way to address your needs, instead using them to establish control and accomplish her objectives. Both kept your actual needs at a distance.

As you offer distinctively Christian care, whether in a formal or informal situation, you'll want to avoid the two extremes illustrated by Eric and Amanda. You need not feel reluctant to use the unique resources of Christianity in your caring, such as asking about spiritual matters, exploring the role of faith in the person's life, sharing a Bible passage, talking about God, and perhaps ending with a prayer or blessing. However, you do need to avoid bombarding individuals with Christian resources without regard for each person's unique situations and needs.

There may be times when providing overtly Christian care would be less appropriate. For example, if someone is skeptical about the Bible, it probably wouldn't help to offer verses from Scripture. In such instances, you might still privately draw on Christian resources, such as praying before and after the visit and trusting God to care for the person you're with, while remaining sensitive about what you say to him or her. However, if the person receiving care is open to Christian resources and could be aided by your sharing them, by all means do so.

FREEDOM TO USE CHRISTIAN RESOURCES

At times you might feel reluctant to use the Christian resources available to you, as Eric was. Here are three reasons why you can feel free to use Christian resources in your caring.

ALL CHRISTIANS ARE CALLED TO CARE

An assumption held by some is that only clergy are qualified to address people's spiritual or religious needs— that only they can appropriately use the caring resources of the faith. This is simply not true. The Bible continually reinforces the concept of the priesthood of all believers, stating that all Christians, regardless of station in life, share with all other Christians the privileges and responsibilities of the faith. For example, see Exodus 19:6, 1 Peter 2:4–10, and Revelation 1:5–6 and 5:9–10.

Whether clergy or laity, you are a part of the priesthood of believers. Christians are called to live out this priesthood by ministering to others, both inside and outside the church. As a Christian, you have some powerful tools available to use in your caring for others, so don't hesitate to call on these resources when appropriate.

THESE RESOURCES ARE THE TOOLS OF OUR TRADE

Another reason you can feel free to use Christian resources is that they are the tools of your trade. Whether you are ordained clergy or not, you are a minister. You have every right to use these tools in providing care. No one thinks it strange when a physician uses a tongue depressor or a stethoscope, or when a dentist uses floss or a mouth mirror. As a Christian caregiver, you need not be reluctant in using the tools of your trade, such as prayer, the Bible, talking about God, and sharing God's forgiveness.

These tools are often appropriate and healthy ways to care for and relate to others. To avoid using the resources of Christianity in an appropriate caring situation would be similar to a physician trying to treat a patient without any medical equipment. It may still be possible to offer some help, but it wouldn't be nearly as effective as it would be with the proper tools.

OTHERS EXPECT YOU TO OFFER SOMETHING DIFFERENT

It can also be reassuring to know that even professional caregivers who do not profess Christianity often recognize the value and validity of a spiritual approach to caring. Helping professionals such as physicians and psychologists generally expect that Christians, ordained and lay alike, will care for people in a distinctly Christian way.

I used to meet each Wednesday over lunch with a group of psychologists, psychiatrists, interns, and residents to discuss and evaluate the latest journal articles and research findings and occasionally hear from guest speakers. One time, we invited a chaplain from the local medical center to speak to the group. During the presentation, one therapist asked the chaplain what unique elements he brought to the healing endeavor. The chaplain said what he offered was distinctive in that he could provide more long-term types of care than the mental health personnel because he didn't have to rotate his clients as much. Someone then asked the chaplain whether he used prayer, Scripture, or other spiritual resources in his care, and his response was, "Well, that's really not my bag."

The psychologists and psychiatrists at the meeting, including those who were not particularly religious, were variously aghast, astounded, and baffled by his answer. They expected that a chaplain's unique contribution would have been to offer spiritual care, and they couldn't imagine why a Christian caregiver would decline to use the tools of that calling. Similarly, those outside the helping professions often consider it appropriate for Christians to use prayer, Scripture, and the like in the course of helping and relating to others.

So don't assume that people will look down on your use of Christian caring resources. When you show your distinctiveness in appropriate, genuine, and effective ways, others will typically respect you for who you are and what you stand for, even if they don't believe as you do.

GUIDING PRINCIPLES

When we use the tools of distinctively Christian care, we want to do so with sensitivity and compassion. Here are two guiding principles to follow when using Christian caring resources.

TREAT PEOPLE AS PEOPLE

First, treat people as people, not as goals or objects. That was one of Amanda's mistakes at the beginning of this chapter: She regarded her care receiver as someone to be influenced and controlled rather than someone who needed genuine respect and care. Treating people as objects is not only bad caregiving; it's bad theology. It fails to meet the hurting person's unique needs and disregards his or her spiritual dignity before God. When a caregiver is concerned more with getting people to accept certain religious views than with helping them find healing and wholeness in God, any attempts at care will be ineffective.

There are many ways—some more obvious than others—of treating a person as an object. For example, one could focus entirely on the person's religious beliefs and overlook the difficult, unaddressed emotions tied to those beliefs. Or one might be preoccupied with sharing preferred Bible verses and prayers, forgetting the need to tailor these resources to the other person's unique situation. Or one could be so intent on sharing personal faith that he or she fails to notice that the other person is not at all ready to hear that kind of testimony.

Here are some questions to ask yourself when using distinctively Christian caring tools:

- Am I genuinely trying to help the other person, or am I trying to accomplish my own objectives?

- Am I using these Christian caregiving tools to fulfill my needs or the needs of the other person?

- Am I demonstrating Christ's love by using these Christian caregiving tools, or am I attempting to gain respect and boost my reputation?

Treating people as people means avoiding ulterior motives and refusing to use others for one's own ends. Instead, it's about focusing on another person's unique needs and helping him or her find hope and healing in Christ.

MATCH RESOURCES TO NEEDS

Second, match the resources you offer to the needs of the person you're caring for. Not every tool will be a perfect fit for every situation. In fact, when Christian resources aren't aligned with the other person's needs, they might hurt more than they help.

Effectively matching caring resources to needs entails doing a lot of listening. Seek to discover and understand the person's needs and life situation *before* doing anything else. In order to use Christian caring tools effectively, you'll first need to listen attentively, explore the other person's frame of reference, and learn what his or her situation and needs are. Then, when appropriate, you can choose distinctively Christian tools that relate directly to the person's unique needs and perspective.

You have the privilege, the right, and the responsibility to be distinctively Christian when you relate to and care for others. The resources at your disposal are not to be ignored, but neither should they be used inappropriately. Learn to use them sensitively and effectively, and they will be a powerful part of your caring toolkit.

PRAYER

Although prayer is an integral part of the Christian life, many Christians struggle to use prayer appropriately and effectively when caring for others. Often, the reason is that they're uncertain as to how to go about it—unsure why they should pray with others, when to pray, how to pray, what to pray about, and even where to pray. Prayer often seems complicated, a specialized skill that might be better left for clergy.

Fortunately, anyone can learn how to use prayer as an effective caring tool. That's what this chapter is all about. Although it focuses on the use of prayer in a more structured caring visit, what it says about prayer also applies to everyday encounters with others.

WHY PRAY WITH OTHERS?

God invites his people to draw near and share their concerns with him by means of prayer. God also specifically calls us to approach him in prayer *together*. James 5:16 urges Christians to "Pray for each other," with the context of the verse clearly showing that it refers to two or more people praying with each other.

We pray for each other not only because God urges it but also because Jesus gives us this promise:

> "Again, I tell you that if two of you on earth agree about anything you ask for, it will be done for you by my Father in heaven. For where two or three come together in my name, there am I with them" (Matthew 18:19–20).

What a powerful incentive to pray together! When you pray with another, God is there too. God has promised to listen attentively to your prayers, understand your needs, and answer your requests. Thus, the motivation for praying with others extends far beyond religious duty or formality.

WHEN—AND WHEN NOT—TO PRAY WITH OTHERS

Prayer is certainly essential to Christian care, but not every moment is the right time to pray with someone you're caring for. Here are some considerations for deciding when and when not to pray.

WHEN IT'S NATURAL

Prayer, when it's offered, should fit in the natural flow of caring and not be tacked on as a routine or obligatory item on a checklist. Because the opportunity for prayer can't fully be predetermined, you'll need to decide during the visit whether to pray and, if so, the best moment for prayer. That determination always depends on the other person's needs, not yours. In other words, pray not when *you* want to or are ready to pray—but rather when the *other person* desires prayer and is ready for it. Careful listening will help you determine when prayer is appropriate.

It's entirely possible that your visit may not include a prayer. That doesn't mean your caring was not distinctively Christian; it's just that the right time to pray didn't come up. The idea is to make prayer a natural part of your conversation, not an intrusion or interruption.

WHEN IT'S WELCOME

While people may generally be open to prayer, it's good to ask whether prayer would be welcome rather than to assume one way or the other. This is especially important if the person is non-religious or not a Christian. The person may well be open to praying, but you'll want to be sure first.

You could simply say something like, "As a Christian, I believe in the significance of prayer, and I would be glad to pray for you, if that's something you would like." In such instances, you would implicitly be offering to pray a Christian prayer, and it's then up to the other person to accept or decline. If the person accepts, you can focus your prayer on any needs he or she has expressed to you. For more on doing this, see "Building a Prayer" later in this chapter.

IN THE CONTEXT OF CHRIST-CENTERED CARE

Prayer together is typically most appropriate after you've done a lot of listening and Christ-centered care, focusing on the process rather than on results. That context reinforces that prayer is a way of bringing a person's needs to God, not a way to inject Christianity into a caring visit where it isn't already present. It needs to be a natural extension of the Christian care that you have offered up to that point. Whether or not you find an appropriate time to pray together, the Christ-centered love and care you show will reflect God's presence in the relationship.

NOT TO SIGNAL THE END OF A VISIT

Although it's common and appropriate to close a visit with prayer, you'll want to avoid the habit of praying *only* at the end of a visit or of using prayer as a subtle signal that it's time to draw the visit to a close.

A danger of always closing with prayer is that the other person might come to see prayer more as a way to say goodbye than as actual communication with God. The person might even feel disappointed when you mention prayer, because it means that you'll be leaving. Using prayer exclusively as a signal that it's time to wrap up diminishes the significance of prayer, both for you and the care receiver.

To avoid this pitfall, remember that prayer can be offered anytime someone has fully expressed a need and a willingness to take it to God together. Make the effort to recognize and embrace those opportunities for prayer whenever they occur.

NOT TO MANIPULATE

Unfortunately, prayer has sometimes been used as a means of manipulating another person into a desired action. For instance, if someone wants a specific person to join a worship team, a manipulative prayer with that person might go as follows:

> Dear God, I come before you with Mary asking that you would give her the desire to be part of the worship team. Give her the courage to get beyond the uneasiness she feels so she can honor and glorify you in this way.

Such an unsolicited prayer is not so much communication with God as an attempt to coerce Mary into joining the worship team. Not only would a prayer of this sort likely fail to produce the desired results, but it would probably also hurt Mary and damage the relationship. That kind of prayer would only be appropriate if Mary had expressed a desire to overcome her uneasiness about joining the worship team. In that instance, the prayer would be coming from her expressed needs, not the ulterior motives of the caregiver.

HOW TO PRAY WITH OTHERS

In many ways, the act of praying with someone else isn't that different from praying on your own, but it does involve a few special considerations.

INTRODUCING PRAYER

Sometimes people feel awkward initiating prayer because they don't know how to do so. Generally, it's best to be assertive in bringing up praying, even as you recognize that the final decision of whether or not to pray is up to the other person. If you sense that prayer would be appropriate, a natural way to introduce the subject is to say something like:

- "Would you like me to pray with you right now?"

- "I'm glad you shared with me some of what you've been feeling. Would it be helpful for us to share these feelings with God in prayer together?"

- "I think you've set a challenging but doable goal for yourself. Would you like for me to pray with you about it to ask for God's help?"

These introductions offer prayer while giving the individual a choice. For prayer to be an effective caring tool, both you and the other person need to be willing to pray together.

ADDRESSING GOD

In prayer of any kind, you begin by addressing God. Remember—and let your prayers show—that God is a loving God who is fully involved in people's lives. Jesus Christ, having shared in all of human experience, truly understands all you talk about when you pray to him. With that in mind, we can and should address God in the way a child would talk to a loving parent.

BEING HONEST WITH GOD

Martin Luther's first rule of prayer is "Don't lie to God." As you pray, seek to be genuine and open. Speak honestly about any anger, sadness, bitterness, fear, pain, or sense of injustice felt by either you or the person you're praying with. Feel free to share every emotion and experience with God. There's no need to clean up your thoughts when praying; God can handle it. God is loving and understanding and wants honesty from us, not nice-sounding yet inauthentic words. Note how honest the prophet Habakkuk is with God:

How long, O Lord, must I call for help, but you do not listen? Or cry out to you, "Violence!" but you do not save? Why do you make me look at injustice? Why do you tolerate wrong? Destruction and violence are before me; there is strife, and conflict abounds. There-fore the law is paralyzed, and justice never prevails (Habakkuk 1:2–4a).

Yet the prophet goes on to say, "The Sovereign Lord is my strength; he makes my feet like the feet of a deer, he enables me to go on the heights" (Habakkuk 3:19). Like Habakkuk, many people find comfort and help in sharing painful moments honestly with God.

CHOOSING MEANINGFUL WORDS

As you pray, be sensitive to the needs and expectations of the other person. Choose language that the person understands and that both of you feel comfortable with. In most cases, you'll want to avoid using highly special-ized religious language, instead favoring everyday words and phrases. At the same time, there's no need to use language that feels out of character for you. People ap-preciate it when you're authentic in your language rather than attempting to use words and expressions you nor-mally wouldn't.

While it's important to choose your words carefully and caringly, try not to be overly conscious of how well you're praying, as if it's a performance. If you stumble or have a hard time finding the right words, just keep going as best you can. Neither God nor the other person will evaluate or judge the eloquence of your prayer. What is most important is that genuine communication takes place.

Paul wrote, "For we do not know what to pray for as we ought, but the Spirit himself intercedes for us with groanings too deep for words" (Romans 8:26 ESV). Many times the best prayer is the one most difficult to express, coming from the heart and reflecting genuine concern. As 17th-century English preacher John Bunyan said, "In prayer it is better to have a heart without words than words without a heart."

WHAT TO PRAY ABOUT WITH OTHERS

Pray about the feelings, situation, or challenge that prompted prayer in the first place. This helps keep the prayer specific and meaningful rather than vague and detached.

It helps to agree together, *before* you pray, about what needs you'll bring to God. Suppose you're visiting a woman named Christina who is facing surgery the next morning. Christina tells you she is worried and afraid. After listening to her, you ask whether she would like to pray, and she says yes.

To ensure you both know what needs should be included in your prayer together, you might then say, "We can ask God to calm your worries and fears for the surgery tomorrow. Is there anything else you would like to express in this prayer?"

When you say this, Christina might respond, "No, that's all I want." Or she might say, "Yes, could we also include my family? I know they're very worried." Whatever the response, you can begin to pray based on those identified concerns, confident the prayer will speak to real needs.

BUILDING A PRAYER

In praying with others, I've found it helpful to use a process of *building a prayer.* That simply means you and the other person discuss what needs to go in the prayer before you start to pray. As you build a prayer, you discover the needs of the individual by inviting him or her to express any and all thoughts, feelings, and concerns. For example, with Christina, your conversation might go something like this:

You: Before we pray, I'd like to know what you're thinking and feeling right now.

Christina: I'm worried that something might go wrong, and I don't know what my family would do if that happened.

You: Tell me more about that.

Christina: I know everything will probably be okay, but . . . well, what if I die?

You: You're worried that you might not make it through the surgery—and about how it would affect your family if that happens.

Christina: Yeah. It's really weighing on me.

You: Maybe we could bring this fear to God in prayer. Is there anything else you would like to share with God?

Christina: No, that's mainly what I'm worried about.

By inviting Christina to share her concerns before you pray, you have sufficient information to build a prayer that meets her needs.

When someone asks you to pray, it might be tempting to immediately fold your hands and begin praying. But remember that caring prayer should meet the other person's needs. A good response might be something like, "I would be glad to pray with you. Before I do, could you share with me what you're thinking and what needs you want me to pray about? That would help me know how best to pray with you."

USING PRAYERS WRITTEN BY OTHERS

In this chapter, I've mostly talked about praying extemporaneously. There are times, though, when using an already-written prayer can help you provide effective care. Here are some suggestions for the use of prayers from books or other resources:

- If you're using a prayer book, become well acquainted with it so you can choose appropriate prayers quickly without searching through the pages while the person is waiting.

- Choose prayers that meet the needs of the individual.

- If the prayer speaks to the person's needs in a general or incomplete way, add a sentence or two that more specifically apply to those needs.

- Read the prayer in a natural voice and at your normal rate. Avoid using a dramatic, preaching voice for this or any kind of prayer. A change in tone can increase the relational distance between you and the other person, adding an impersonal quality to the prayer.

- The Psalms are a great resource for prayer. Again, it helps to become familiar with them through study and personal meditation so that you can choose a psalm appropriate to a person's needs without taking too much time.

- The Lord's Prayer can apply to a vast range of situations, either by itself or with another prayer. One advantage is that because it's so well known, the other person may be able to join you in saying it.

WHERE TO PRAY WITH OTHERS

You can pray together anywhere, provided you adjust your style of prayer to the surroundings. A visit in a private home can be especially conducive to quiet moments of prayer, but prayer can also be appropriate in a public place like a hospital. If you're in a place where there's a lot of activity and little privacy, such as a waiting room, you might ask whether the person would like to pray then and there or find a different place or time.

Even in a hospital room there may not be total privacy. If another patient is in an adjoining bed, you might want to adjust your style by praying more quietly with the person you are visiting. Make sure your attention and ministry stay focused on the person you came to visit.

WHAT IF THE PERSON DECLINES PRAYER?

Most often, people will welcome the suggestion to pray with them. Occasionally, though, the other person may decline, possibly giving a reason.

One reason for declining could be that the person has already prayed extensively about the matter and doesn't feel an immediate need to pray further. If so, honor the other person's wishes, remembering that praying together is about the other person's needs, not yours.

Another reason for saying no could be that the person doesn't feel deserving of prayer. Resist any temptation to brush off how the person feels and pressure him or her into praying, which would be uncomfortable and unhelpful for him or her. Instead, give the person a chance to talk about those feelings.

For example, a person who is going through a bitter, painful divorce may say something like, "I'm too embarrassed to pray. I don't think God will listen to me." You might respond by saying, "I appreciate your sharing that with me. How are you feeling right now?" Such a response shows genuine concern and a willingness to relate to the person's feelings. Keep in mind too, that the individual might feel more open to prayer later.

People may also say no because they prefer to pray privately and are unsure about praying with someone else. In these instances, you may want to share why you value praying together. If you do so, be sure to respect the other person's feelings, avoid applying guilt or pressure, and remember the final decision on whether to pray together is the other person's.

One more reason people might say no to prayer together is because they simply don't like to pray. Although you know how beneficial prayer is, you can't force another person to value prayer as you do—and applying pressure often leads to results opposite from what you intend. The best you can do is respect the other person's wishes and patiently continue to care.

Whatever reason people have for declining to pray with you, there's no need to be defensive or see it as a personal rejection. As your relationship continues, there might be other occasions when the person will feel more open to prayer. Be patient, pray privately for the other person, continue to focus on the process of offering distinctively Christian care, and trust God for the best possible outcome.

Prayer is our response to God's gracious invitation, based on the needs of the other person, and a confident expectation that God will act. As you provide distinctively Christian care, both you and those you pray for will find strength and assurance, knowing that your concerns are left in the hands of our loving God.

THE BIBLE

Many of the guidelines for prayer covered in the previous chapter also apply to the use of the Bible in caring relationships. As with prayer, any sharing of Bible verses or stories needs to be *welcomed* by the other person and to fit naturally into the conversation. Just as you'll choose prayers to meet a person's specific needs and concerns, so you'll focus on sharing biblical principles and passages that speak to those needs and concerns. This chapter focuses on *why* and *how* you can use the Bible effectively in your caring relationships.

WHY USE THE BIBLE?

The Bible is an excellent caring ministry resource because it records how God has ministered to the needs of people through the ages. The Scriptures are a written witness of God's marvelous, unceasing love.

Through the Bible, we see how God sent his Son Jesus to become human so he could bring love, healing, hope, forgiveness, and new life to us: "For God so loved the world that he gave his one and only Son, that whoever believes in him shall not perish but have eternal life" (John 3:16). As the people we're caring for experience bad news in life—conflict, suffering, illness, tragedy, grief—they could use the Good News. They could use the gospel.

The Bible addresses a wide range of human concerns, experiences, and situations. When people are experiencing problems and needs, they can turn to Scripture for the reassuring words and promises of God. For example, the Psalms run the gamut of human emotions, from despair to exhilaration, from anger at God to love for him. Jesus' parables capture essential truths that enrich our spiritual life. The lives of biblical figures provide examples of God's faithfulness and guidance in the midst of human weaknesses and struggles. The teachings of the Bible guide people in the art of living in relationship to God, one another, and ourselves.

As Christian caregivers, we use the Bible in caring for others because it contains an important message for everyone. We use the Bible because it's practical, dealing with real concerns all people may have. We also use the Bible because it's *alive:* "For the word of God is living and active" (Hebrews 4:12a). The Bible works in the hearts of believers for good.

HOW TO USE THE BIBLE EFFECTIVELY

This is not to suggest that caregivers should always use the Bible at length or force it into every encounter. As effective as a particular medication may be, a physician still wouldn't prescribe it for every type of illness. In caring for others, how you use Scripture is important.

CHOOSING A TRANSLATION

There are a wide variety of translations of the Bible to choose from. They range from those that strive for precise, word-for-word equivalence with the original languages to those that aim to accurately convey the thoughts and concepts through contemporary words and phrases.

Most of the time, it's perfectly all right to use the translation you prefer or the one used by your congregation. However, if you know that someone has a preference for another translation, it would be thoughtful and caring to use that translation if possible. A good way to confirm this is to simply ask, "Is there a specific translation of the Bible you prefer?"

KNOWING PASSAGES AHEAD OF TIME

In order to use the Bible effectively, it's helpful to know some passages that are relevant to typical caregiving situations. Having appropriate passages in mind beforehand allows you to more quickly and easily match Scripture with the person's needs.

You can begin by keeping a list of potentially helpful caregiving passages, drawn from your own reading and from others. You might ask the people you care for whether any verses are especially significant for them. Not only will that equip you to be a better caregiver to them, but it will also give them the chance to take a more active role in the caring relationship.

LISTENING FIRST

While your sharing from the Bible can be very meaningful for someone receiving care, it's important to not rush to the Scriptures prematurely. Otherwise, the other person might feel as though you're glossing over his or her situation or pushing for a specific kind of response.

Before you even consider sharing Scripture, you'll first want to do a lot of listening to understand the person's unique situation, communicate empathy, and let him or her know that you're fully present. Then, once the other person knows he or she has been heard, you might offer to share a Bible verse or story that suits the circumstances.

INTRODUCING SCRIPTURE

When you think it would be helpful to refer to Scripture, you might say something like:

- "Listening to you talk about how your feelings of grief are gradually being replaced by warm memories, I'm reminded of Jesus' promise: "'Blessed are those who mourn, for they will be comforted'" (Matthew 5:4)."

- "Something that really spoke to me when I was in a situation similar to yours is the story of the death of Lazarus, where it says, 'Jesus wept' (John 11:35). It helped me realize that if Jesus could cry with grief, it was certainly all right for me to do the same."

- "You've mentioned how much you appreciate the Psalms. Would you like to read Psalm 121 with me? It's given me hope in the midst of personal difficulties, and maybe you'll find it helpful too. It reminds me that God is always with me and is my protector."

Sometimes people wonder what they should say after sharing a selection from the Bible with someone. It may be that no further comment is necessary, since a passage might have spoken clearly and directly to the person's need. If you have a few thoughts that could help the person consider the passage further, you might briefly share them. You can also simply ask, "Do you have any thoughts or feelings that you'd like to share?"

It may be that you and the other person want to spend a good amount of time discussing a particular passage, especially if it very clearly addresses the needs of the individual. In this kind of discussion, do a lot of listening—possibly listening more than 75 percent of your time with the other person—and avoid lecturing. This will help ensure that your discussion meets the needs of the other person. Any comments you do offer about the passage should be focused on helping the person explore the passage for him- or herself.

The Bible should never be used to harass, manipulate, or shame someone. Instead, you'll share the Bible to bring reassurance, to deepen understanding, and to strengthen the other person's relationship with God in the midst of his or her current situation.

THE GIFT OF FORGIVENESS

It's no secret that we fall short of God's original design for us. Through our thoughts, words, and actions, all of us sometimes cause legitimate offense to others and to God. If we didn't, there would be no need of forgiveness.

When we behave in ways that offend or hurt others, we damage our relationship with them. Such offenses can create distrust, leading those involved to build walls to cut themselves off from one another. The only thing that can tear down those walls is the gift of forgiveness.

If forgiveness is important in our human relationships, it's even more so when it comes to our relationship with God. People sometimes assume their offenses against God are so great that they cut off any possibility of a meaningful relationship. In fact, the opposite is true. God possesses infinite grace, mercy, and love, and his response to our sin is to offer full forgiveness through Jesus Christ, granting us the opportunity to have an eternal relationship with the Father, Son, and Holy Spirit.

Forgiveness is a universal need. Many people, including those you may care for, struggle with feelings of guilt and don't know what to do about them. Although there's little you can do to secure forgiveness for someone from other people, you can do something about his or her feelings of guilt before God.

One of the great privileges and responsibilities for all Christians is to bring God's offer of forgiveness and grace to those who need to hear and experience it. Sometimes when a person is wrestling with guilt, God's forgiveness can seem distant and vague. Hearing someone communicate that gift in an empathetic, accepting way can help make the offer warm, personal, and real. Your ability to share the forgiveness of God with others is one of your most valuable tools as a Christian caregiver. While there will certainly be times when you need to forgive someone who has hurt you, this chapter focuses on talking about forgiveness with someone whose words or actions may have hurt people other than you.

THE NATURE OF FORGIVENESS

Forgiveness makes it possible to connect deeply not only with God but also with other people. It tears down walls and restores broken relationships. Martin Luther King Jr. described forgiveness in this way:

> Forgiveness does not mean ignoring what has been done or putting a false label on an evil act. It means, rather, that the evil act no longer remains as a barrier to the relationship. Forgiveness is a catalyst creating the atmosphere necessary for a fresh start or a new beginning. It is the lifting of a burden or the cancelling of a debt.[1]

The ongoing process of forgiveness means continually setting aside the obstacles that create relational distance between ourselves and others.

Forgiveness is a prerequisite for caring. Because past wrongs can create relationship barriers, even when those wrongs haven't directly affected you, it is difficult to care for another without forgiving and removing those barriers. Someone may have done something seriously wrong or hurtful, but God still calls you to forgive the person and demonstrate your willingness to forgive by accepting him or her.

Forgiving someone does not require that the person first confess his or her sin to you; it is possible to forgive unilaterally. One powerful example of unilateral forgiveness is Jesus on the cross: "Jesus said, 'Father, forgive them, for they do not know what they are doing'" (Luke 23:34a). Another is Stephen: "Then he fell on his knees and cried out, 'Lord, do not hold this sin against them'" (Acts 7:60a). Forgiving in this way provides an opportunity for healing to take place in the relationship.

This is not to say that confession of sins is optional or unimportant. True healing occurs only when the care receiver recognizes his or her mistake. This is why it's important for the caregiver to be patient and listen, helping the other person explore any existing issues, before introducing the subject of forgiveness. But you don't have to wait until someone confesses a sin in order to have a forgiving, accepting attitude. An attitude of forgiveness often leads to confession and repentance because it provides freedom for the other person to take an honest look at how his or her actions have affected others.

The Christian forgiveness you share with others is distinct, based on Jesus' life, death, and resurrection. It is forgiveness that restores people's relationship with God and provides new hope in their relationships with others. Thus, there is tremendous power and depth in the forgiveness you share with those weighed down by brokenness and guilt.

SHARING FORGIVENESS

Here are some practical ways to introduce forgiveness into your relationships.

ACCEPTANCE

First of all, make forgiveness evident by accepting the care receiver as he or she is. Show that the other person does not have to meet any standards to earn your acceptance.

Acceptance is vital in setting the stage for meaningful forgiveness to take place. By setting no conditions before caring, loving, and forgiving others, you avoid taking the relationship down the wrong path. As a caregiver, you'll want to avoid acting in a way that implies non-acceptance of the person.

Communicating acceptance does not mean you overlook or approve of the attitudes and actions of others. Rather, it means that you accept people as they are, recognizing that they are made in God's image.

LISTEN

When people want to let out their feelings of guilt, take the time to listen to what they're saying and feeling before you share God's forgiveness. Resist the temptation to speak a forgiving word prematurely without hearing everything the other person is trying to say. Only by listening fully and helping someone see the consequences of his or her actions can you truly help bear the other person's burdens.

When forgiveness is shared too quickly, it is rendered meaningless. Dietrich Bonhoeffer calls this "cheap grace."[2] People need to come to terms with their guilt, and self-examination and confession take time. If people haven't yet come to see their need for forgiveness or expressed all they feel guilty about, any forgiving words will seem irrelevant or impertinent. They're likely to think, *You can't possibly forgive me! You don't know half the story!* or, *Why are you forgiving me? What did I do wrong?* For a person to experience forgiveness fully, you'll need to provide sufficient time and accepting love.

This does not mean you should *withhold* words of forgiveness from others. It means that before you share God's forgiveness, it's important to listen fully to them and help them unload their burdens of guilt, rejection, failure, and sin.

SHARING WORDS OF FORGIVENESS

After listening to people's feelings and allowing them to unburden themselves, you will want to share the gospel message of forgiveness. How exactly you offer these words of forgiveness depends on you, the other person, the situation, and the person's need.

You might want to share a brief statement about God's love through Christ for that individual in spite of his or her sin. You could say something like:

I'm glad you were willing to talk about this. I know it can be painful to share openly and honestly like that. I want you to know that God loves you and forgives you for your mistakes.

Or, you could turn to a passage or story in the Bible that proclaims God's forgiveness:

Sometimes it's hard to believe that our sins could ever be forgiven. But God has promised to be right there with us even when we find it difficult to forgive ourselves. The Bible tells us, "If we confess our sins, he is faithful and just and will forgive us our sins and purify us from all unrighteousness" (1 John 1:9).

There is no more exciting or life-transforming news to share with people than that God has forgiven them. Again, this news should be shared with care and only after plenty of listening. Yet, if the need is there, be certain to share words of forgiveness. Your responsibility is to provide the very best care for others, and there is nothing better than forgiveness in Christ.

HOW—AND HOW NOT—TO APPROACH FORGIVENESS

To illustrate how forgiveness functions in a caring relationship, here are three examples of different ways to approach the same situation. The first two examples illustrate how *not* to approach forgiveness, while the third shows the way forgiveness should function in a caring relationship. Bear in mind that these examples are somewhat exaggerated and abbreviated.

Suppose a man named James has recently gone through a divorce. About a month before the divorce was finalized, James's children spent the weekend at his apartment. He spent a lot of time unjustly criticizing and undermining his wife in front of the children, and since then the children have been disrespectful and disobedient to their mother. Now, four months later, James is feeling guilt over his actions. In looking for someone to talk to about this, he turns to three friends.

HARSH HARRY

The first friend he approaches is Harsh Harry.

James: You know about my divorce, Harry, and—well, something's really been bothering me. A few months ago, I had the kids over for the weekend, and I must have spent the entire time criticizing Madeline to the kids. I said some stuff that was exaggerated and not really true. Since then, they've been really disrespectful toward her. I just don't know what to do.

Harry: James, how could you do that? You know you shouldn't have turned them against Madeline!

James: I know, and I feel terrible about it. When Madeline called, she was livid. She said, "What did you do to those kids?" I mean—

Harry: Well, I don't blame her.

James: I guess I'm looking for some help or guidance. I just don't know what to do. You're my friend—what do you think?

Harry: I don't have anything to say until you realize exactly what you've done.

James: I do understand, and I'm really sorry for doing it. I wish I could go back and change it.

Harry: Well, you can't. It's done. Have you repented? Have you asked God for forgiveness?

James: I've tried. I know I'm not going to do it again, and I want to make up for it. I just feel so ashamed, I don't know how to talk to God about it.

Harry: You need to tell God what you did, say you're sorry, and ask him to forgive you, and you need to do it right away.

Harsh Harry is not allowing any *real* confession to take place. Harsh Harry deals with the problem in a superficial way, pressuring James to feel guilty and to hastily speak words of repentance. He makes forgiveness dependent on words correctly spoken while neglecting James's inner struggle.

One risk of this heavy-handed yet surface-level approach is that James might give in just to get Harry off his back. That would be unfortunate, because James would be pretending to have feelings he didn't have. At best, James's expression of repentance would be external, not a matter of the heart.

Another risk is that James might feel defensive under the bombardment of Harry's criticism. Were this to occur, James might be driven to justify behavior he is inwardly ashamed of, and nothing would change about his situation.

LENIENT LARRY

The second person James talks to is Lenient Larry.

James: There's something that's been bothering me lately. A while back, before the divorce, I had the kids over for the weekend. I spent the whole time badmouthing Madeline to the kids—I said a number of things that just weren't true. I feel awful.

Larry: Oh, I'm sure it wasn't that bad. Besides, I can understand how you'd say things like that. You had been through a lot. I wouldn't dwell on it.

James: But I talked to Madeline, and since that weekend, the kids have been constantly disobedient and disrespectful to her because of what I said.

Larry: She's probably exaggerating. They might have made a comment or two, but she's blowing things out of proportion. Besides, you're not responsible for what they do when they're with her.

James: You may be right, but I know I said some untrue and hurtful things about her to the kids.

Larry: So you made a mistake. I think that was just a normal reaction on your part, don't you? You're being too hard on yourself. What's done is done—you need to move on.

James: I guess, but—

Larry: Besides, as Christians, we need to remember that God forgives us our sins. Whatever happened, you're certainly forgiven for it.

James: I suppose so. . . .

Lenient Larry demonstrates a major pitfall in a caring relationship: not allowing any real confession or expression of *realistic* feelings of guilt. James was carrying a garbage bin filled with refuse. Instead of helping James empty out the garbage and clean the bin, Larry took some cheap cologne and sprayed it on top. Because Larry erred by announcing forgiveness prematurely, James would leave this encounter carrying a superficially sweet-smelling bin, still full of garbage.

CARING CARY

The third person James speaks with is Caring Cary.

James: I need to get this off my chest. The kids stayed with me for a weekend about four months ago, before the divorce. That whole weekend, I was venting about Madeline to them. I said things about her that weren't true and blew other things out of proportion. One harsh word led to another, and it got out of control.

Cary: You couldn't resist the temptation. Then, once it started, you couldn't stop.

James: Exactly! And the worst part is that since then, they've been disrespectful toward Madeline all the time. I was really unfair to her, and the kids actually believed me!

Cary: You see yourself as causing this.

James: Yes. I realize that as Christians we're forgiven for things like this, but what I did—I'm not usually like this. I don't want to hurt Madeline or interfere with her relationship with the children. That wouldn't be good for anyone.

Cary: I can tell you're feeling angry at yourself. You know what you did was hurtful.

James: I know, but still, I wonder if I'm being too hard on myself. What's done is done, and I can't go back and change it, so maybe I should just move on.

Cary: I don't think it's that simple, James. What you said may be in the past, but the effect it had is still real and ongoing. It's something that still needs to be dealt with.

James (after a long silence): You know, you're right. I really messed things up. I just don't know where to turn or what to do.

Cary: Have you said anything to God about all this?

James: Yes, I told God I was sorry. I said I acted wrongly and thoughtlessly.

Cary: Do you believe God has forgiven you?

James: I guess so. I'm having a little trouble really accepting that, though. I bet God thinks I'm terrible. I bet you do too.

Cary: I don't think you're terrible at all, and neither does God. You've done something that hurt Madeline and your children, and it's important to recognize that and address the situation, but God forgives our sins, and I'm sure he's forgiven you.

From there, the conversation continues with James and Cary exploring what James might do to rectify the situation with his children and ex-wife.

Caring Cary was characterized by *balance.* He was willing to sit down with James and listen to him without condemning or glossing over what happened. Recognizing that James was offering his own confession, Cary didn't try to take over and push him into confessing in a particular way. Note also that when James started to drift into rationalization, Cary gently and firmly got James back on track. Although definitely caring, Cary certainly recognized the seriousness of the situation and didn't try for a quick fix.

Cary's approach was the most effective and lasting in helping James move toward true forgiveness. By not rushing in too quickly and short-circuiting James's confession, Cary demonstrated real care for how James was feeling and avoided cluttering up the conversation with timeworn clichés or magical formulas. Caring Cary demonstrated the proper way to talk about forgiveness.

FORGIVING YOURSELF

Finally, I want to touch on the topic of self-forgiveness. Many people find it easier to forgive others than themselves. As Christians who care, though, it's important that we accept that God forgives us, just as certainly as he forgives everyone else. By recognizing that we're forgiven ourselves, we can experience peace and become better able to share God's forgiveness with others.

In his book *The Wounded Healer,* Henri Nouwen notes that since we are part of a broken world, everyone suffers from wounds of loneliness and alienation, makes mistakes, and has a variety of shortcomings. Yet, Nouwen says that our wounds can be turned into sources of healing as we recognize that pain and suffering come from the depth of the human condition—and that healing comes only when Christ enters those depths.

This means that being human is both our greatest resource and greatest liability. We can be creative and spontaneous, and we can make mistakes. We can be empathetic and caring, and we can be self-centered and oblivious to others. Only when we recognize and accept that we aren't perfect can we honestly and humbly demonstrate humanness. When we do so, care receivers can relate to us more easily because they're more comfortable connecting with someone who comes across as fully human, genuine, and humble.

As caregivers, we also benefit from not being under the pressure to do everything perfectly, allowing us to be more relaxed and work more effectively. Falling into the perfectionist trap would result in our focusing more on our own needs so that we become wrapped up in self-evaluation and neglect our care for others.

In order to avoid the dangers and pitfalls of perfectionism, we need to forgive ourselves for the inevitable mistakes we make. We need to recognize our mistakes and shortcomings for what they are. At the same time, we need to recognize that God has already forgiven us.

You are free from your sins. You have a real basis for forgiving yourself: God has already done so.

SHARING A BLESSING

Chapter 6 noted that you might want to use prayer at different times during a caring visit rather than always at the end. Another distinctively Christian resource, however, would be used mainly for the end of a visit: a blessing or benediction.

The Latin root of *benediction* simply means "well-saying." In this sense, benedictions or blessings are also common in everyday life:

- "Have a great day."

- "See you later."

- "Take care."

These are all benedictions of a sort; they're ways of conveying the hope that all might go well with the other person after you part. Even the most common, everyday benediction has religious roots—*goodbye* comes from a contracted form of "God be with you."

There is an important difference, however, between these benedictions and distinctively Christian ones. "Take it easy," "Have a good one," and "Take care" all imply action on the part of the other person, as though that person were responsible for the day going well. Christian benedictions contain no such expectation; instead, they are expressions of faith that the day's outcome is in God's hands.

God's presence and activity is the foundation of the Christian benediction:

- "The *Lord* bless you . . ."

- "The grace of our *Lord Jesus Christ* . . ."

- "The peace of *God* . . ."

These are all expressions of God's grace. *You* don't bless you; God blesses you. A Christian benediction proclaims that God has you in his care and constantly watches over you. In this sense, such benedictions are *remembering tools.* They remind the giver and the recipient alike that God is present and in charge. Christian benedictions bring comfort by sharing God's promises and assuring people that God will continue to be at their side. In offering a benediction, you can make the presence of God even more real to the other person. In essence, you're saying, "I'm leaving, but you are not left alone."

HOW TO BLESS

As with other Christian caring resources, timing is important for delivering God's blessing. Often, blessings or benedictions are most appropriate at the close of a visit, although it's possible that a blessing may be called for at some other time. You might also determine that a blessing is inappropriate in certain situations, such as when the other person is not comfortable with an overtly Christian expression. Before offering a blessing or benediction, ask yourself: *What is the other person's need? Would a blessing be appreciated and natural at this time?*

When you decide it might be appropriate to use a benediction, you could lead into it by saying, "Before we go, if you'd like, I could share a blessing with you." Then, wait for the other person to confirm that a blessing would be welcome.

Depending on your relationship with the other person, you might consider the possibility of offering physical touch as well. You could say, "Do you mind if I hold your hand or put my hand on your arm for a moment? I'd like to share a blessing with you." Your touch can be a natural, meaningful expression of your presence as you approach God together to receive the gift of his love. Touch can be especially beneficial for those whose other senses are diminished, such as by age, infirmity, or heavy sedation. However, if either you or your care receiver would feel uncomfortable with touch, you're better off not doing it. Any reluctance or discomfort on the part of one person can detract from the blessing.

THE FORM OF THE BLESSING

The form of your blessing will probably vary from one situation to another. Use whatever blessing is most appropriate for the caregiving circumstances.

Formal, stylized benedictions, such as those used at the close of worship services, can be a great comfort when the other person is familiar with them. It can help to write out one or more possible benedictions to carry with you or possibly memorize. Here is a sampling of some of the more familiar biblical benedictions you might use or adapt:

- The Lord bless you and keep you; the Lord make his face shine upon you and be gracious to you; the Lord turn his face toward you and give you peace (Numbers 6:24–26).

- May the grace of the Lord Jesus Christ, and the love of God, and the fellowship of the Holy Spirit be with you all (2 Corinthians 13:14).

- And the peace of God, which transcends all understanding, will guard your hearts and your minds in Christ Jesus (Philippians 4:7).

- May the God of peace, who through the blood of the eternal covenant brought back from the dead our Lord Jesus, that great Shepherd of the sheep, equip you with everything good for doing his will, and may he work in us what is pleasing to him, through Jesus Christ, to whom be glory for ever and ever. Amen (Hebrews 13:20–21).

Informal or extemporaneous benedictions can also be appropriate, especially in situations where a formal benediction could seem a bit out of place—for example, over a cup of coffee in a restaurant. Informal benedictions can be specifically tailored to a person's needs and thus might at times be even more meaningful than formal benedictions. Here are some examples:

"Allison, may God shower you with blessings as you move to a new town and begin a new job. May a sense of God's presence be with you always."

"Daniel, may God hold you in his arms in the midst of your loss, bringing you peace and comfort."

"May Jesus watch over you and keep you in his care as you recover from illness, and may you always be aware of his presence and help."

Shorter blessings might be appropriate as well:

- "God be with you."

- "God bless you."

- "Peace and joy to you."

- "Peace be with you."

The situation, the person's needs, and your own preference will determine your choice of benediction. Whether you decide to offer a blessing formally or informally, briefly or at greater length, speak with conviction. Benedictions are not casual goodbyes said halfway out the door; nor are they stiff formalities for concluding a visit. When you feel personally assured the person is in God's hands, that assurance will come across in the blessing you speak.

Finally, I'd like to share with you a benediction that's one of my favorites because of its emphasis on the whole person:

> May God himself, the God of peace, sanctify you through and through. May your whole spirit, soul and body be kept blameless at the coming of our Lord Jesus Christ. The one who calls you is faithful, and he will do it (1 Thessalonians 5:23–24).

A CUP OF COLD WATER

For many people, the abundance of cool, clean drinking water is a fact of life that we rarely even think about. In ancient Israel, though, the availability of water was never taken for granted. The dry climate made it necessary to treasure and protect every available water resource. Some people were fortunate to live near a river or lake where they could collect water in jars. Others dug wells to tap into underground springs or streams. Still others relied on cisterns or reservoirs to collect rainwater.

Even though water was scarce in ancient Israel, the most basic act of hospitality and kindness for a guest was to offer a cup of cold water. It's in this context that Jesus introduces another distinctively Christian caring resource:

"And if anyone gives even a cup of cold water to one of these little ones because he is my disciple, I tell you the truth, he will certainly not lose his reward" (Matthew 10:42).

When motivated by Christian faith, hope, and love, a simple act like offering water to someone who is thirsty is distinctively Christian care.

THE MEANING OF A CUP OF COLD WATER

Sometimes, the offer of care might be a literal cup of cold water. However, what Jesus said applies equally to *any* act of kindness or comfort, no matter how small, that's offered out of Christian love and refreshes another person or meets a genuine practical need. We can think of actions like these as cups of cold water:

- giving someone a ride
- running an errand
- offering a blanket
- cooking or helping with a meal
- doing the laundry or helping with other household chores
- providing childcare
- watching a pet while someone is out of town

- helping out with yard work or gardening

As with any other Christian caring resource, it's important to first make sure that the other person is open to and would welcome the cup of cold water. For example, you could say something like, "It's a little chilly in here. Would you like me to find you a blanket?" Asking first provides the assurance that the other person will benefit from and welcome what you're offering.

WHAT SANCTIFIES A CUP OF COLD WATER

What *sanctifies* an act of kindness? In other words, what makes a cup of cold water holy and distinctively Christian? Simply put, an act of kindness is sanctified when it's done in God's presence, in the power of the Holy Spirit, and as an expression of the love and compassion of Jesus. Any time you express Jesus' love in a way that meets people's needs, you are providing Christian care.

God's presence and active involvement makes every aspect of your care Christian from the start. This is true whether or not you offer distinctively Christian words along with a cup of cold water.

To be sure, praying, sharing Scripture, speaking words of forgiveness, talking about God, and exploring someone's spiritual concerns are all important acts of care. Yet Jesus indicates that your caring can be Christian without specifically mentioning God, Christ, the Holy Spirit, the

Bible, or the church. Whatever form your caring takes, when God's love flows through you to another person, you are being distinctively Christian.

Of course, there are times when you'll have an opportunity to share about your motivation for offering a cup of cold water. By all means, take those opportunities when they occur, but remember that your words don't sanctify your caring actions—God does.

People frequently draw a sharp distinction between *sacred* and *secular,* as if God is heavily involved in some things and not at all in others. The truth, though, is that God created everything and is involved in every part of his creation. God claims all of life, including what we call the secular. Jesus doesn't stand on the sidelines, waiting for us to use the right words before he steps in. He's always present and already at work in the middle of the situation before we arrive.

The idea to keep in mind is this: *By virtue of whose you are and what motivates you, any caring or relating you do is distinctively Christian.*

THE UMBRELLA OF CARING

I like to envision the entirety of Christian caring as an umbrella. That umbrella covers varied aspects of care, such as prayer, talk about God, using the Bible, and cups of cold water. Using resources like prayer and Bible reading is important—and so is giving a cup of cold water. It doesn't have to be an either/or proposition, and it shouldn't be. You'll offer both a cup of cold water *and* outwardly Christian resources, depending on the other person's unique needs at the time. Both types of resources are distinctively Christian tools. Both have their place.

Attempting to care for others without ever appropriately using the Bible and prayer is like trying to swim with both arms tied behind one's back, and using such resources while consistently neglecting opportunities to give a cup of cold water is a mere caricature of Christian ministry. When care is limited to one approach or the other, it's less than complete Christian care.

Effective Christian care requires more than words. It requires a heart filled with faith, hope, and love, reflected in acts of kindness and comfort.

THE EVANGELISM–CARING CONNECTION

There is a strong, often unnoticed relationship between genuine Christian caregiving and effective evangelism. Each includes and builds on the other; evangelism involves Christian care, and Christian care arises from the good news of Christ.

Unfortunately, the word *evangelism* evokes mixed emotions. For some, it is positively associated with sharing the message of God's love and redemption. For others, the mention of evangelism evokes guilt because they think they aren't doing enough to spread that message. For still others, the term is negatively associated with extreme, overzealous behavior that pressures people to believe or act a certain way.

Given the varied reactions to evangelism as a word and a concept, it's important to explore exactly what true evangelism is and how it connects with caring.

THE MEANING OF EVANGELISM

Evangelism is the act of bringing good news to someone. The ancient Greek word *evangelion* was used to refer to the news of a battle won or of a fallen enemy. When Roman emperors came to power, they would commission evangelists to travel throughout the empire and announce the "good news" of their ascent. The writers of the New Testament chose this familiar word to describe the activity of telling others about Jesus—spreading the news that God sent his Son to offer forgiveness, hope, and new life to the world through his life, death, and resurrection.

At its heart, then, Christian evangelism is offering good news—in fact, the best possible news. Unfortunately, Christians have too often taken a heavy-handed approach to evangelism, which can lead people to react to the gospel with guilt, defensiveness, or rejection rather than joy and acceptance. In order to really connect with someone, the evangelistic message needs to be communicated in a loving, compassionate way, inviting the other to truly experience the good news of Jesus Christ. That's why the evangelism–caring connection is so crucial.

This chapter looks at how evangelism and caring are related and how providing good care helps Christians to be effective evangelists. True Christian evangelism is always caring, and distinctively Christian caring is a vital aspect of evangelism.

EVANGELISM IS CARING

At its core, evangelism is a caring act because the message we proclaim brings genuine hope and healing. What greater gift could we share with others than love and life in Jesus Christ? When we tell someone what Jesus has done for us, we show that we truly care about the other person. We show interest in him or her as a whole person.

Effective evangelism relates the gospel person to person in a way that demonstrates the love and care of Christ. It involves relating warmly and personally as one who has been touched by God's redeeming love.

The reality that evangelism is caring has two important implications.

- *First, love is a vital motive for evangelism.* It's important to continually evaluate what leads you to tell someone about Christ. Is it about trying to fulfill a duty, gain church members, or check off another item on a spiritual checklist? Or is it based on a genuine desire for the other person to know and experience the love of Christ? St. Paul writes, "If I speak in the tongues of men and of angels, but have not love, I am only a resounding gong or a clanging cymbal" (1 Corinthians 13:1). One could just as easily say, "If I speak all the right words of evangelism, but have not love, I am only making meaningless noise." If your evangelism is to be effective, its emphasis needs to be on caring for the person.

Now, growing church membership and attendance are important because they can indicate that effective evangelism is taking place. Yet Jesus' call to love one another must always be the starting point for evangelism.

- *Second, evangelism is conversation, not lecture.* At times, people have unfortunately thought that doing evangelism means giving the other person a well-prepared monologue. But caring evangelism takes place in conversation, not lecture. When you truly care about someone, you'll want to not only communicate your message to that person but also listen to him or her. You'll want to know what the person is thinking, feeling, believing, and experiencing. Once you've had a chance to get to know the person and demonstrate your care and concern, the message you share can be in response to the other person's actual needs, rather than what you initially assumed he or she needed.

The importance of evangelism as conversation is amply illustrated throughout the New Testament. It's why Jesus proclaimed the good news differently to Nicodemus (John 3) than he did to the Samaritan woman (John 4). It helps us understand the interaction between Philip and the Ethiopian eunuch (Acts 8) and the way Peter relates to Cornelius and his household (Acts 10). From the beginning, evangelism was intended to occur through conversation. Your words will be most meaningful and effective when you first take time to listen and understand.

In the process of evangelism, your role is to love the other person and, when the opportunity presents itself, to share the good news of the forgiveness, hope, and healing found in Christ. It's not your responsibility to change the other person's mind or heart. Once you've done what you can to share the gospel, you trust God for the results.

CARING IS EVANGELISM

Not only is evangelism caring, but caring is also a part of evangelism. At first glance, they might appear to be two entirely separate, independent activities. Certainly, many caring people aren't Christian, and even Christians frequently offer care without specifically mentioning God or their faith. Thus, caring in and of itself might not seem to witness to the love of Jesus Christ.

But Christian caring is evangelistic, because being Christ to people prepares them to hear the good news. Caring for someone involves meeting the needs of that whole person. Through actions of love, God reaches down and touches people with his power. His healing activity can renew all aspects of an individual's life. Our caring provides a channel through which God's love can and does flow; our loving words and actions concretely demonstrate the good news.

This is particularly true of a good caring relationship. A quality Christian caring relationship is a true embodiment of the gospel, communicating God's life-transforming love. God's mercy and grace are powerfully demonstrated in such relationships.

Christian caregivers thus *incarnate* and live out the Christian message. Through your caring, you make the Christian message tangible—something that can be seen and touched. You give flesh and bone to God's Good News.

Caring is evangelism when your care actively *reveals* Jesus Christ. This does not mean that words are unimportant, but what you say and do need to be aligned. Together they constitute a dynamic whole that the Holy Spirit can use to transform people's attitudes and beliefs, helping them to be made whole themselves.

Good evangelism and good caring are inseparable, embodying each other. Evangelism demonstrates a love for people, and a love for people demonstrates the good news of Jesus Christ. The way to make this happen is by actively building a relationship with someone in need of the hope and healing God offers. May the Lord enable us all to carry out the task at hand.

CELEBRATE RESULTS—BUT FOCUS ON THE PROCESS

Helping people through challenges in their lives is rewarding. When you're caring for another person, it feels good to be able to say, "Jen is beginning to live again in the midst of her grief," or "David is finally able to move forward after the loss of his job." Those kinds of results are genuinely worth celebrating when they occur.

It's important to be careful, though, as looking at specific results in the context of distinctively Christian caring risks shifting the focus excessively toward results. As mentioned in chapter 1, a results-oriented approach hinders caring. It can be nonproductive—or even counterproductive—for caregivers and care receivers alike.

When people agree to receive care from someone, often they are focused on results themselves—that's why they're accepting care in the first place. One of our first tasks as caregivers is to help people toward a productive perspective on results. Fixation on results is so common that this principle can't be overemphasized: *Results start happening when you stop pushing for them!*

Goals are helpful, and good things can happen when Christians provide care. Yet, as described and demonstrated throughout this book, your main focus as a caring individual needs to be on the process of caring rather than on results.

PROCESS GOALS VS. RESULTS GOALS

Process goals differ from results goals as verbs differ from nouns. Kindling a fire is a process; a fire is a result.

Suppose you befriend Jen, whose husband has died. You hope that through your caring relationship with Jen, she will work through her grief and find a new sense of normal more quickly and effectively than she would have otherwise. These are admirable ends that just about anyone would hope for when helping someone stricken by grief.

In your caring for Jen, however, there are two very different ways you could proceed—one way that works and another that doesn't. You could focus on the process of caring for her, or you could focus on the results of caring. Here's what some process goals and results goals for relating with Jen might look like.

Process Goals	Results Goals
1. Provide a safe, accepting environment for open conversation about Jen's loss.	1. Jen will no longer feel her loss as a raw, painful wound.
2. Ask good questions that explore any difficult feelings Jen might have, such as sadness, hurt, or anger.	2. Jen's sadness, hurt, and anger will dissipate.
3. Give Jen your full attention.	3. Jen will know you care for her, trust you, and begin to trust others as well.
4. Discuss Jen's fears about returning to her job and how she might handle offers of sympathy.	4. Jen will return to her job and deal successfully with people's offers of sympathy.
5. Help Jen think through the challenges and opportunities of entering into social situations without her husband.	5. Jen will get out, socialize, and participate in church and community activities.
6. Communicate to Jen that it's acceptable and healthy to grieve.	6. Jen will work through her grief.

Note that each of the process goals begins with a verb indicating something *you* can do as a caregiver. The results goals, meanwhile, begin with a noun—specifically, *Jen*—and indicate something she would do or some way she would change. All the results goals are beneficial, but they are beyond your direct control. Each is the outcome of a process. You won't get lasting results without going through a process to get there. And if your eye is fixed on the outcome, you're likely to overlook the process altogether. Focusing directly on *results,* then, could slow down growth and healing or even prevent it.

Many a sports team has lost because the players were distracted by thinking about the championship game while they were still early in the playoffs. By focusing on the outcome of winning the championship, they failed to follow the necessary process that would lead them to that result. That's why an effective coach helps players focus on the game at hand—and on the current moment within that game—rather than anything that might happen in the future. The team needs to keep its attention on the many actions necessary to perform. In the case of basketball, for example, that includes good dribbling, good passing, playing tight defense, and taking good shots. Victories are results of many actions well executed—in other words, *a process.*

THEOLOGICAL IMPLICATIONS

For the Christian, the distinction between process and results is even more significant. The most important results, including the healing that takes place through caring, are ultimately out of our hands; these results are primarily what *God* accomplishes, not what we ourselves bring about. Scripture directs us to the *process* of Christian living, through which God works:

- Be transformed by the renewing of your mind (Romans 12:2a).

- Do everything in love (1 Corinthians 16:14).

- We can comfort those in any trouble with the comfort we ourselves have received from God (2 Corinthians 1:4).

While you are engaged in the *process,* you work under the promise that "he who began a good work in you will carry it on to completion until the day of Christ Jesus" (Philippians 1:6). For the Christian, this *process* paves the way for *results.*

The theology of process and results has several implications for your care. First, you rely upon God for results. Ultimately all results of caregiving are in God's hands. He decides the nature and extent of the healing. You are called to trust in God and in his transforming presence.

Second, because you realize that God will provide healing in the future, you can focus fully on the present. Jesus tells Christians, "'Therefore do not worry about tomorrow, for tomorrow will worry about itself'" (Matthew 6:34a). Given the assurance of God's loving presence and healing power, you are free to give yourself completely to the caring process.

Third, you can truly view yourself as an instrument of God, a part of God's process of healing. This understanding is foundational to your identity as a Christian caregiver.

DISTINCTIVELY CHRISTIAN RESULTS

What follows are some distinctively Christian results that often develop when you focus on the caring process. Every situation is different, but those you are caring for are likely to experience results like these at different times and in different ways.

COMMUNITY

For many people, receiving distinctively Christian care during a difficult time may be their first taste of genuine Christian community—of God's people loving, encouraging, and supporting one another. As people see and experience for themselves the value of this community, they may become increasingly open to connecting with it in a stronger, more meaningful way.

SELF-AWARENESS

Working through difficult thoughts and feelings with a Christian caregiver can often help suffering people take a giant step forward in understanding themselves, including their unique background, personality, experiences, and ways of relating. That growing self-awareness may help them find healing and navigate life more effectively.

PERSEVERANCE

As Christian caregivers provide much-needed support, hurting people may find the perseverance they need to endure and move beyond the current crisis. What may once have seemed unbearable or impossible becomes more doable with someone to walk alongside them. That doesn't mean everything becomes easy for them, as the situation may continue to be very difficult, but they now might be able to see their way through, not only in the immediate situation but also in the face of future challenges.

FREEDOM FROM GUILT

The caring process can help people become increasingly open to God's mercy and grace when guilt is burdening them. As they receive the unconditional positive regard of the caregiver, they may become better able to accept God's love and forgiveness, empowering them to move beyond possible feelings of guilt. Receiving God's forgiveness can also open the door for people to receive forgiveness from others—and from themselves—freeing them from guilt so they can move into the future.

FREEDOM TO FORGIVE

Besides receiving forgiveness themselves, those receiving care might grow in the desire and ability to offer forgiveness and mercy to others. Learning to forgive others for past wrongs can help heal relationships while freeing people from holding on to and feeding negative feelings.

REBIRTH AND RENEWAL

Christian caring often leads people to experience a new or refreshed relationship with God. Those who didn't have faith in Jesus Christ can come to know the joy of Christian rebirth thanks to the care they received in a time of need. Or, those who have professed faith but began feeling distant from God may experience again how much God loves and care for them, leading to a renewal of their relationship with God.

FAITH

Through the process of Christian care, hurting people may experience a new or growing belief that God is attentive to them and at work in their life and the world. As they see Christ's love through their caregiver, along with genuine changes in their life, their faith in God grows. This faith in turn helps them better cope with the ordinary and extraordinary challenges they may face.

HOPE

Christian hope is both in the present and for the future. The source of this hope is the knowledge that Jesus is with each Christian "'always, to the very end of the age'" (Matthew 28:20b). Those who have received Christian care might display, through their attitudes and expectations, a deep trust in Christ's continuing presence and eventual return.

LOVE

As people receive the love of God, their heart may begin to change so that they grow in their ability to love God and others. God's love for them fills their heart, overflows, and pours out to the people around them. As they grow in love, they learn to prioritize and seek to meet others' needs rather than just their own.

TRUST IN GOD AND OTHERS

According to psychologist Erik Erikson, the first developmental crisis people undergo at an early age is building a sense of trust. Trust enables us to believe that others will be there for us when we need them. Many hurting people struggle with trust, wondering whether they can count on God or others to be there, with them and for them, in the crises of their life. Through the care of a trustworthy, distinctively Christian caregiver, they may begin to rebuild their trust in God and others.

CHRIST-CENTERED SELF-IMAGE

When people receiving care believe that they are precious to God and that the Holy Spirit dwells in them, they can gain a much healthier ego and self-image. They draw their self-worth and identity not from fleeting accomplishments or the approval of others but from the enduring truth of being a child of God. This is not haughtiness or conceit; it is feeling good about oneself because Jesus Christ is alive and well within.

GREATER WHOLENESS AND PEACE

As a result of Christian care, hurting people can come to experience God's peace and stability. Rather than being merely the absence of hostility or a state of inner contentment, this peace is the sense of wholeness, stability, and well-being connoted by the Hebrew word *shalom.* When people experience this true peace, their relationships become whole and complete—with others, with God, and with themselves.

A PERSPECTIVE ON RESULTS

This list certainly does not include every distinctively Christian result. Nor does it include all those results of caring that are good but are not specifically Christian in character—for example, comfort expressing one's feelings, greater honesty with oneself and others, overcoming painful emotions, or reducing anxiety. However, it does give a picture of the kinds of positive outcomes that can occur when we focus on the process of providing care.

The results of Christian caregiving also have to do with *you the caregiver* and the strengthening of your own personal faith and Christian life. The more you use the tools of your trade, the more your faith in God will grow, and the better care you'll be able to provide.

Results are certainly great, but they belong to God, who chooses to let you share in the pleasure of them. Don't chase them; let God send them to you. Expect and celebrate results, but don't fixate on them. Be glad when they come, but don't spend a lot of time trying to figure out how to make them come or when they're going to begin. Stay true to the process and rely on God's timing. Count on the certainty that the Lord's sense of timing and purpose is better than anyone's. Rely on the promise of the Lord in Revelation 21:5: "'I am making everything new.'" Now that's what I call results!

HOPE-FULL CAREGIVING

Hope is one of the most distinctively Christian resources a caregiver can offer. The uniqueness of Christian hope is that it comes directly from God. Having Christian hope means that we don't have to place our trust solely in human capacities, institutions, or ideals. Instead, our hope is in God, who is actively at work in both the caregiver and care receiver and who brings true healing and wholeness.

Because Christian hope rests securely on God, it encompasses the present and future. This is clearly demonstrated in Jesus' raising of Lazarus:

> "Take away the stone," he said. "But, Lord," said Martha, the sister of the dead man, "by this time there is a bad odor, for he has been there four days." Then Jesus said, "Did I not tell you that if you believe, you would see the glory of God?" So they took away the stone. Then Jesus

looked up and said, "Father, I thank you that you have heard me. I knew that you always hear me, but I said this for the benefit of the people standing here, that they may believe that you sent me." When he had said this, Jesus called in a loud voice, "Lazarus, come out!" The dead man came out (John 11:39–44a).

Jesus' prayer is a clear demonstration of hope that embraces both the present and the future, the *now* and the *not yet*. The words used by Jesus indicate his deep knowledge that God would answer his prayer—that, in a sense, God had already raised Lazarus from the dead. This is genuine, God-given hope: trusting God for the future in the present.

In your Christian caring, you can rest in the assurance that there is One greater than you and greater than any difficult circumstances the person you're caring for may be facing. This One is working through you to produce the same assurance and hope in the other person, both for the now and for the not yet. The individual may be struggling and hurting in the present, but he or she can also trust that God is not finished working in his or her life. Even when setbacks and disappointments come in the *now,* you and the care receiver can choose to trust in God's *not yet* and embrace Christian hope for healing.

As a distinctively Christian caregiver, you can demonstrate God's hope for the person you're caring for and be a tangible expression of God's presence. Here are eight practical ways you can become an instrument through which Christian hope can flow into others.

BE CONSISTENTLY SUPPORTIVE

A potent way to express and instill hope is by communicating through your words and actions that you will consistently support the other person in the midst of his or her struggles. By staying with the person through thick and thin, you help him or her feel safe, secure, and not alone.

BE AVAILABLE

Hope is also fostered by letting people know they can get in touch with you as necessary, especially in an emergency. It's reassuring to another to know that someone cares enough to be available should the need arise. Occasionally, you might run into someone who takes advantage of this privilege, but rather than try to limit your caring relationship with qualifiers in advance, it's better to deal with such situations gently and firmly if and when they occur.

EMPATHIZE

As described in chapter 4, empathizing is about connecting with another person and his or her challenges without making those challenges your own. It's a way to reach into the mudhole and help the other person out while maintaining the stability needed to avoid falling in yourself. Just knowing that there's someone who understands—and who is willing and able to offer a helping hand out of the mud—offers real hope to a person in need of care.

ACCEPT THE PERSON

Another way to instill hope is by communicating through words and actions you unconditionally accept the person you're caring for. Acceptance leads to trust, and trust is closely followed by hope.

If a person makes a potentially shocking statement such as, "I hate my mother—I wish she were dead," there are non-accepting and accepting ways to respond.

Non-accepting: "That's terrible! You should never say that!"

Accepting: "It sounds like you're dealing with some serious anger toward your mother. *(Pause)* Let's talk about that."

Accepting doesn't necessarily mean agreeing with particular thoughts and feelings or encouraging the other person to continue thinking and feeling that way. It simply means acknowledging that you understand and believe the other person is experiencing those thoughts and feelings—and that you still accept him or her. Jesus communicates acceptance despite people's difficulties and sin, and you can help others find hope by doing the same.

HELP OTHERS SEE THE POSITIVE IN THEMSELVES

Sometimes those who are struggling find it difficult to discover or accept any good in themselves. Their inability to manage their difficulties may leave them with harsh feelings toward themselves, thereby completely overshadowing the talents, skills, and positive traits they possess. You can help instill hope in someone by giving permission and gentle encouragement to see his or her own positive qualities.

This is precisely what Jesus did when Nathaniel was brought to him. He said, "'Here is a true Israelite, in whom there is nothing false'" (John 1:47). Jesus could have said, "Here is a sinner who needs repentance!" In this instance, though, he chose to accentuate the positive.

Note that this is different from pressuring others to be positive about themselves or their situation. That kind of pressure typically just leaves people feeling worse. Instead, after doing a lot of listening, give them the opportunity to notice and accept what is positive about themselves.

POINT OUT OPPORTUNITIES FOR GROWTH

Making space for the positive includes, by implication, recognizing that no one is all positive—that being human means everyone has weaknesses and limitations. Rather than taking those apparent negatives as cause for discouragement, one can look at them through the lens of hope and see opportunities for growth and healing.

Jesus often praised Peter but did not hesitate to rebuke him when necessary. He spoke the truth in love to Peter about his forthcoming denials (John 13:36–38) and then graciously restored Peter following the resurrection (John 21:15–19). Discussing with another his or her faults and limitations may at times be bad-tasting medicine, but it can bring the hope of future healing in those areas. You can take heart that your own weaknesses are opportunities for God's strength to show itself, and you can lovingly communicate the same vision to another.

ACKNOWLEDGE JESUS' PRESENCE

At all times, recognize that Jesus is with both you and the one you're caring for, and help the other person recognize his presence. Jesus' supportive presence provides true, lasting hope for you and the other person. He is before you to lead you. He is behind you to guard you. He is beside you to support and comfort you. He is above you to bless you. When you recognize and acknowledge Jesus' presence, you can confidently tell and show the person that he is with and for you both.

BE DISTINCTIVELY CHRISTIAN

Finally, you can instill hope simply by being distinctively Christian. By speaking and relating in a Christian manner, you convey your competence as a Christian caregiver, providing the hope that Christian care aims for. This book as a whole shows ways you can consistently do that in your caring.

These practical ways to bring hope to a person in need have a common thread: They ask you to imitate Jesus. Christ is a consistent source of support for you. Christ is available to you. Christ empathizes with you. Christ accepts you, freeing you from judgment. Christ helps you recognize the positive within you. Christ strengthens you to confront your weaknesses and limitations. Jesus Christ is in you, with you, above you, beside you, behind you, and for you. And so you can be Christ to others through your distinctively Christian caring.

CALLED TO CARE

Excellent caregiving happens in many arenas. Healthcare professionals tend to a host of physical ailments. Mental health professionals address issues of mental and emotional distress. And you are equipped with the unique tools of Christian caring and increasingly aware of the distinctive nature of your calling. Your unique vantage point in this hurting and broken world gives you an important role along with all other healers and helpers. They are doing excellent and necessary work, and so are you.

POWER AND POTENTIAL

Remember whose power you bring into every situation: the power of God the Father, his loving Son, and the Holy Spirit.

Remember also the tools that draw on God's power: the Bible, prayer, forgiveness, servanthood, hope, and other distinctively Christian resources.

To me, the power of God and the potential of these resources are deeply reassuring and motivating.

- I am relieved that my calling is to be a caregiver, while God is the Curegiver.

- I feel a sense of partnership and security, knowing that God is fully present with me and the other person.

- I have purpose and direction because I know the One who motivates me, where I come from, and where I'm going.

- I feel more competent because I have tools like prayer, Scripture, and blessings to draw on whenever they're needed.

- I feel inner warmth and awe when I'm privileged to relate to people's deep spiritual needs.

- I am free to go the extra mile with those who need me, maintaining a healthy Christian perspective on servanthood.

- I rejoice that the "cups of cold water" I give to others are welcomed by God as distinctively Christian caring.

- I draw courage from the long line of faithful tradition in which my caring stands, realizing that I'm continuing the work of God's people throughout the ages.

INTEGRATING THEOLOGY AND PSYCHOLOGY

Throughout this book, I've been asserting the need for unique and distinctive Christian caregiving. Now I'd like to share a little more of my own background to help clarify my interest in the theme.

My education was split between two streams. I went to a Christian elementary school, high school, college, and seminary. At the end of that, I was pronounced ready to be a pastor. In addition to my theological training, I received a Ph.D. in clinical psychology, which was for the most part nonreligious education and training. At the end of four years, I was pronounced ready to be a psychologist.

None of that training had prepared me to integrate the two streams of theology and psychology. Because my psychological training was almost totally nonreligious, though, I think I developed an even greater appreciation for the power and possibilities of the spiritual combined with the psychological. Psychology makes a substantial contribution to the well-being of people. So does theology. When the two are joined in a practical and healthy union, the possibilities are boundless.

In this book, my intent has been to take you well beyond theorizing about the integration of psychology and theology. Christianity is, after all, practical. Its exercise, benefits, and demands begin not in the promised future but in the here and now. I hope these pages have provided you with confidence, inspiration, and excitement about *your* potential for unique and distinctive caring as a Christian, with the insights of both psychology and theology guiding you.

YOUR CAREGIVING JOURNEY

Now is the time for action. Your caring journey will be the result of God's call and your own distinctive gifts. I'm privileged to have been a part of your journey thus far, and I'm hopeful for what the rest of your journey will bring. My prayer is that you have found in this book an empowering resource for being distinctively Christian in your caring.

May the peace and joy of almighty God the Father, the Son, and the Holy Spirit go with you.

NOTES

CHAPTER 1

1 J. P. Louw and E. A. Nida, eds., *Louw-Nida Greek English Lexicon of the New Testament Based on Semantic Domains,* 2nd ed. (New York: United Bible Societies, 1988), s.v. "therapeuo."

CHAPTER 2

1 Henri Nouwen popularized this term in his classic book *The Wounded Healer* (New York: Doubleday, 1972).

2 Brother Lawrence, *Practicing the Presence of God,* trans. Robert Edmondson (Brewster, MA: Paraclete Press, 2007), 20–21.

CHAPTER 3

1 The book *Don't Sing Songs to a Heavy Heart: How to Relate to Those Who Are Suffering,* available from Stephen Ministries, explores in greater detail what to say and what not to say when someone is struggling with life difficulties.

CHAPTER 4

1 Martin Luther, *The Freedom of the Christian: Annotated Study Edition* (Minneapolis, MN: Fortress, 2016), 488.

2 Carl R. Rogers, "The Necessary and Sufficient Conditions of Therapeutic Personality Change," *Journal of Consulting Psychology* 21:2 (1957), 99.

CHAPTER 8

1 Martin Luther King Jr., *A Gift of Love: Sermons from Strength to Love and Other Preachings* (Boston: Beacon Press, 1963), 47.

2 Dietrich Bonhoeffer, *The Cost of Discipleship* (New York: MacMillan, 1963), 45.

ABOUT THE AUTHOR

Rev. Kenneth C. Haugk, Ph.D., is a pastor, clinical psychologist, author, and teacher. He received his Ph.D. in clinical psychology from Washington University and his M.Div. from Concordia Seminary, both in St. Louis, Missouri.

Dr. Haugk is the founder and Executive Director of Stephen Ministries St. Louis. As a parish pastor, he discovered that the needs for care in and around his congregation exceeded what he alone could provide. Drawing on his background in psychology and theology, he trained nine members of his congregation as lay caregivers, called Stephen Ministers, to work with him in providing one-to-one care to hurting people in the church and community. This caring ministry was so well received that in 1975 he started the Stephen Ministries organization in order to equip people to begin and lead it in other churches. Since then, over 13,000 congregations and other organizations have started Stephen Ministry, and more than 750,000 Stephen Ministers have been trained to provide care to those experiencing difficult times in life.

Over the years, Dr. Haugk has written books and courses on a variety of caring and equipping topics, such as *Speaking the Truth in Love, Discovering God's Vision for Your Life, Don't Sing Songs to a Heavy Heart, Journeying through Grief,* and *Cancer—Now What?* He has also published widely in psychological journals and popular periodicals.

Dr. Haugk has received numerous awards, including the National Samaritan Award from the Samaritan Institute for significant contributions to the field of caring ministry. He is a frequent conference and workshop speaker on topics such as caregiving, grief, dealing with cancer, spiritual gifts, conflict resolution, and leadership.

Ken lives in St. Louis, where he enjoys playing basketball and tennis, rooting for the Cardinals, and spending time with his two daughters, son-in-law, and three grandchildren.

STEPHEN MINISTRIES

Stephen Ministries is an international not-for-profit Christian educational organization founded in 1975 and based in St. Louis, Missouri. Its mission is:

> To equip the saints for the work of ministry, for building up the body of Christ, until all of us come to the unity of the faith and of the knowledge of the Son of God, to maturity, to the measure of the full stature of Christ.
>
> *Ephesians 4:12–13*

The 40-person staff of Stephen Ministries carries out this mission by developing and delivering high-quality, Christ-centered training and resources to:

- help congregations and other organizations equip and organize people to do meaningful ministry; and

- help individuals grow spiritually, relate and care more effectively, and live out their faith in daily life.

Best known for the Stephen Ministry system of lay caregiving, Stephen Ministries also publishes books and conducts seminars on a variety of topics, including grief, assertiveness, dealing with cancer, spiritual gifts, leadership, and crisis care.

A number of these resources are described on the following pages. To learn more about these and other resources or to order them, visit stephenministries.org or call (314) 428-2600.

Don't Sing Songs to a Heavy Heart: How to Relate to Those Who Are Suffering

Pastors, lay caregivers, and suffering people alike have high praise for *Don't Sing Songs to a Heavy Heart* by Kenneth Haugk, a warm and practical resource for what to do and say to hurting people in times of need.

Forged in the crucible of Dr. Haugk's own suffering and grief, *Don't Sing Songs to a Heavy Heart* draws from his personal experience and from extensive research with more than 4,000 other people.

For anyone who has ever felt helpless in the face of another person's pain, *Don't Sing Songs to a Heavy Heart* offers practical guidance and common-sense suggestions for how to care in ways that hurting people welcome—while avoiding the pitfalls that can add to their pain.

With its combination of sound psychology and solid biblical truths, *Don't Sing Songs to a Heavy Heart* provides a wonderful follow-up to *Christian Caregiving—a Way of Life*.

Cancer—Now What?
Taking Action, Finding Hope, and
Navigating the Journey Ahead

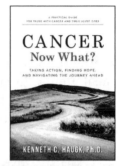

Cancer—Now What? is a book to give to people with cancer and to their loved ones, helping them navigate the medical, emotional, relational, and spiritual challenges they may encounter.

In writing the book, Kenneth Haugk drew on everything he learned as he walked alongside his wife, Joan, during her battle with cancer. He built on that foundation by conducting in-depth research with thousands of cancer survivors, loved ones of people with cancer, and medical professionals, incorporating their wisdom, experience, and expertise.

The result is a comprehensive, easy-to-read how-to resource, written in a warm, conversational style and covering a wide range of topics relevant to individuals and families dealing with cancer.

People who give the book to those affected by cancer include friends and relatives, pastors and congregations, oncologists and other physicians, cancer centers and hospitals, businesspeople and professionals of all kinds, and many others. For anyone wanting to support and encourage someone after a cancer diagnosis, giving a copy of *Cancer—Now What?* is a simple, powerful way to help.

A *Giver's Guide* is also available, which provides ideas for giving the book to those with cancer and their loved ones.

Speaking the Truth in Love: How to Be an Assertive Christian

This book invites the reader to live assertively—just as Jesus did. Building on a scriptural understanding of assertive living, it shows the reader how to develop healthy relationships with others—one to one, in small groups, in task-oriented teams, and in congregations.

This deeply spiritual and extremely practical book makes clear:

- what assertiveness is (and is not)
- the Biblical foundation for assertiveness
- how Jesus is our model for living assertively
- how to be assertive in prayer and praise
- how to make, refuse, and negotiate requests
- how to express and receive compliments
- how to handle criticism, anger, and other tough relational issues

You will learn practical ways to relate to others with greater honesty, compassion, and respect. Experience the freedom and joy of Christian assertiveness!

Journeying through Grief

Journeying through Grief is a set of four short books that individuals, congregations, and other organizations can share with grieving people at four crucial times during the first year after a loved one has died.

Book 1: *A Time to Grieve,* sent three weeks after the loss

Book 2: *Experiencing Grief,* sent three months after the loss

Book 3: *Finding Hope and Healing,* sent six months after the loss

Book 4: *Rebuilding and Remembering,* sent eleven months after the loss

Each book focuses on the feelings and issues the person is likely to be experiencing at that point in their grief, offering reassurance, encouragement, and hope. In *Journeying through Grief,* Kenneth Haugk writes in a warm, caring style. He shares from the heart, drawing on his personal and professional experience and from the insights of many others. The books provide a simple yet powerful way to express ongoing concern to a bereaved person throughout the difficult first year.

Each set comes with four mailing envelopes and a tracking card that makes it easy to know when to send each book.

Also available is a *Giver's Guide* containing suggestions for using the books as well as sample letters that can be personalized and adapted to send with them.

Antagonists in the Church: How to Identify and Deal with Destructive Conflict

Antagonists are individuals who, on the basis of nonsubstantive evidence, go out of their way to make insatiable demands, usually attacking the person or performance of others. These attacks are selfish in nature, tearing down rather than building up, and are often directed against those in a leadership capacity. (From chapter 2, "What Is Church Antagonism?")

Pastors, church staff, governing boards, lay leaders, and others will find the insights, principles, and practical methods offered by this book valuable for identifying and dealing with individuals who attack leaders and destroy ministry—as well as for creating a congregation environment that prevents future attacks.

The *Study Guide* turns the book into a course to equip a group of church leaders to effectively deal with and prevent antagonistic attacks. It includes discussion questions for each chapter, which help course participants apply the strategies and concepts to their own unique situations.

Stephen Ministry

Stephen Ministry is a complete system for training and organizing laypeople to provide one-to-one Christian care to hurting people in the congregation and community.

Stephen Leaders—pastors, staff, and lay leaders—are trained to begin and lead Stephen Ministry in the congregation.

Stephen Leaders, in turn, equip and supervise a team of Stephen Ministers—congregation members who provide ongoing care and support to people experiencing grief, divorce, hospitalization, terminal illness, unemployment, loneliness, and other life difficulties.

As a result:

- hurting people receive quality care during times of need;
- laypeople use their gifts in meaningful ministry;
- pastors no longer are expected to personally provide all the care that people need; and
- the congregation grows as a more caring community.

More than 13,000 congregations and organizations from more than 180 denominations—from across the United States, Canada, and 30 other countries—have enrolled in Stephen Ministry so they can more effectively provide Christ-centered care to people in need.

Christian Caregiving—a Way of Life is one of the books Stephen Ministers read during their initial training.